ARGUMENTS FOR LIBERTY

A Libertarian Miscellany

Second Edition

ARGUMENTS FOR LIBERTY

A Libertarian Miscellany

Second Edition

J C Lester

The University of Buckingham Press

First published in Great Britain in 2011
This second edition published in 2016
by

The University of Buckingham Press
Yeomanry House
Hunter Street
Buckingham MK18 1EG

© J C Lester

The moral right of the author has been asserted.

All rights reserved. No part of this publication may be reproduced, stored or introduced into a retrieval system or transmitted in any form or by any means without the prior permission of the publisher nor may be circulated in any form of binding or cover other than the one in which it is published and without a similar condition including this condition being imposed on the subsequent purchaser.

A CIP catalogue record for this book is available at the British Library

ISBN 978-1-908684-62-2

Printed and bound in Great Britain by
Marston Book Services Ltd, Oxfordshire

To David, Sarah, Meg and Will
Four delightfully civilised friends

Contents

Preface to the second edition ix
Preface to first edition xi
1) Libertarianism: an Extremely Short Introduction 1
2) My Greatest Fear: the State 7
3) The Good, the Bad, and the Neutral: Abortion 10
4) Murder, and Child and Animal Abuse 16
5) The Pure Joy of Heroin 21
6) The Ulster Nation: Troops Out, Market In 25
7) Ulster: Cut the Apron Strings 33
8) AIDS: Not "Everyone's Problem" 40
9) The Market for Justice 44
10) Market Libertarianism Entails Quasi-Contracts 46
11) Glib Glossary: a Random and Ironic Guide to Social Thought 49
12) The Market for Free Speech (or 'Free Speech: is Rushdie for it?') ... 53
13) The Right to Private Discrimination 56
14) Free Trade in Human Body Parts 58
15) No Representation Without Taxation! 60
16) Civil Society and Civil Liberties: Two Statist Views Reviewed 63
17) Libertarian Controls on Guns, Drugs, Prostitution, Etc. 66
18) Anti-Libertarianism: a Book Review 70
19) Behind the Caricature: Reply to a Befuddled Author 72
20) Right to Roam or Licence to Trespass? 77
21) The Disability Studies Industry 83
22) What's Wrong with "What's Wrong with Libertarianism" 95
23) A Sceptical Look at "A Skeptical Look at Karl Popper" 102
24) Statement on the London Bombings 108
25) Nozick's Flawless Libertarianism? A Book Review 110
26) An Attack on the Realm: a Book Review 116
27) A Plague on Both your Statist Houses 124
28) Smoking and Libertarianism: a reply to Amartya Sen 133
29) The Political Compass and Why Libertarianism is not Right-Wing 135
30) Against *Against Intellectual Property* 148
31) A response to "Libertarianism and pollution" 155
32) IP, the NAP, and Pre-Propertarian Liberty 160
33) Afterword and Further Reading 184

Preface to the second edition

This edition contains three new chapters and many minor revisions.

What is libertarianism? There is no essential meaning of any mere word such that other uses must be objectively and crucially mistaken. It is far more important that we have debates about real problems and how to solve them. However, the ideology of libertarianism is a fairly specific thing and not a mere word. And in order to clarify any debates, it seems worth pointing out what that ideology is and some apparent errors and confusions about it. For some texts appear to be unwittingly uninformed or muddled rather than intentionally different.

Libertarianism is, more or less, the view that 1) interpersonal liberty (in some sense of people not initiating constraints—or proactively imposing—on each other) is an overridingly desirable goal, and 2) this is best promoted by having a minimal state (minarchy) or no state at all (anarchy). Classical liberalism (as opposed to the completely muddled sense of modern 'liberalism') is less precisely and less universally pro-liberty. But some early classical liberal texts are minarchist or anarchist, although most are not. Hence libertarianism is probably best seen as a proper subset of classical liberalism. All this ought to be fairly clear and yet it does not always seem to be understood, even among many self-identified libertarian texts.

There are various examples in various combinations. Some texts assume that liberty is a zero-sum concept such that if one person has more liberty, then another person necessarily has less: that proactively imposed slavery is simply the slave-owner having more liberty at the slaves' expense. This flouts the standard libertarian view that such a slave-owner is exercising aggressive power. Some texts, implicitly or explicitly, assume that liberty is not really the desirable goal but, instead, non-aggression, or self-ownership, or (natural) rights, or a system of (natural) property, or the free market, or some combination of these things (or, at best, they have an intuition that conflates or confuses these things with liberty but they have no proper theoretical explanation). Some texts assume that libertarianism is vague enough to include state tax-transfers for welfare, such as a basic income guarantee. Some texts assume that (state-enforced) resource-egalitarianism is compatible with or even implied by libertarianism. Some assume that—whether as history, social phenomena, or theory—classical liberalism and libertarianism are completely identical or, conversely, completely separate from each other. If texts explain libertarianism in any of these potentially confusing ways, then they and their critics ought at least to be aware of how different what is being said is from the basic account above.

There is a slight ambiguity in the title of this book. "Arguments for Liberty" might be read in two ways. One way is simply that the arguments are on the side of liberty rather than against liberty (as in a debate). That is the sense that is intended. The other way is that the arguments are supposed to offer epistemological support for liberty such that the nature and desirability of liberty becomes something stronger than a conjecture. As it is not logically possible to transcend a conjectural framework (or web of assumptions) to reach something stronger, that sense is not intended. The ambiguity might have been avoided by making the title "Arguments in Defence of Liberty" or even "Arguments in Defence of the Libertarian Conjecture". But the increased wordiness did not seem worth it. In any case, most justificationists would notice no ambiguity because they would typically conflate the two senses (thinking that an argument on the side of liberty must be offering support) and most critical rationalists would already know better. Moreover, the relevant contents of the book are clear enough on this epistemological matter.

Preface to first edition

This book contains sundry libertarian scrivenings produced over around thirty years, and very lightly edited here. They should each have some individual interest in their own way, and together they also function as a miscellaneous introduction to libertarianism at varying levels of breadth and depth, and from the populist to the scholarly, and from the orthodox to the heterodox. As all these pieces were written independently of each other, there is both occasional repetition and even inconsistency (and any cited internet links were valid at the time and might not be now). But the observant reader might notice change and development in these ideas over time.

Several of the given dates are estimates. The first two pieces are the most general in scope to help the uninitiated reader to have an overview of libertarianism. The succeeding articles are approximately chronological until the penultimate one which is an explanation of libertarianism's place on the overall Political Compass (or Map) and an attempt to determine the reader's position on it by way of a brief quiz. But there is no reason not to dip into whichever chapters might take one's interest first of all.

1) Libertarianism: an Extremely Short Introduction

(The pre-Bowdlerised chapter published in *A Beginner's Guide to Liberty*, 2009.)

The word 'liberty'

The words 'liberty' and 'freedom' are not usually distinguished in any systematic or significant way. They simply have different roots in the English language. 'Liberty' has its origins in the Latin 'libertas'. 'Freedom' comes from the Old English 'freodom'.

It is usually not necessary to discuss what we mean by a particular word. We can take it for granted that others mean the same thing as we do. But this is not always true with the fundamental words that arise in moral, social and political contexts. One such ambiguous and disputed word is 'liberty'. So it is necessary to give some kind of definition or even theory of 'liberty' before we can say clearly why it is important.

'Liberty' in its most general sense refers to the absence of constraints on something. Here we are interested in the absence of constraints on people by other people. There are two main ways to interpret this, which we can call zero-sum liberty and non-invasive liberty.

Zero-sum liberty

With zero-sum liberty, one person's loss of liberty is always another person's gain in liberty. If someone takes my car without my permission, then I lose the liberty to use that car and the taker gains the liberty to use that car. This has implications that can be used as criticisms. 1) Such liberty cannot be maximised for all, it can only be competed over or shared in some way. 2) Competing over liberty does not sound desirable, but is even equality of such liberty much better? What exactly does it mean? Why is it desirable? Does it require continual political intervention to enforce the equality? 3) In any case, it follows that the standard for what types of liberty matter (liberty to do this but not liberty to do that) must be something other than liberty. But why can't a conception of liberty itself be a standard of what is allowable? 4) This view means that we have to balance the 'liberty' of a thief, or other aggressor, against that of his victims. Do we really think that this is what we are, and ought to be, doing? The zero-sum conception of liberty gives us problems rather than solutions. Yet people do sometimes talk of liberty in this way (even some libertarians).

Non-invasive Liberty

Non-invasive liberty agrees with the popular view of liberty as not being interfered with, or not being proactively imposed on, by other people. Not being attacked or robbed is part of liberty; attacking or robbing people is not part of liberty. And this has implications that look more like solutions than problems. 1) In principle, anyone in a society can have complete liberty. 2) In principle, everyone in a society can have complete liberty at the same time. 3) A clear and crucial distinction is now possible between (non-invasive) liberty and (invasive) licence. We can say that a thief, or other aggressor, is exercising licence and not liberty. And those who resist an aggressor (or use coercion to recover restitution from an aggressor) are merely protecting their own liberty, not limiting the (non-invasive) liberty of the aggressor. 4) Such liberty is not only desired by everyone but is generally also thought desirable for everyone, at least to a large degree.

External property ownership and even self-ownership itself are consequences of maximising non-invasive liberty. Therefore, expressed in more practical and plain terms, 'liberty' means being able to do what you like with your own body and your own property (as long as you are not thereby proactively imposing on the body or property of others). This sense of 'liberty' is what libertarians, or classical liberals, usually mean when they advocate liberty. This is also the dominant conception of liberty within Western history and it applies to any society that is described as generally 'liberal'. It is the importance of this liberty that we are explaining.

Limits on liberty?

Don't states, or governments, need to provide some vital legislation and tax-funded services? The radical libertarian answer is that the state provides nothing useful that liberty cannot provide better—by free choices, free markets and charity. People are the best judges of how to lead their own lives. And the free market, without the state, uses the price system to guide scarce resources into their most productive uses. Where people agree that help is needed, charity is more efficient and libertarian than state hand-outs.

By contrast, political intervention will inevitably be economically arbitrary and also invasive. It is arbitrary because the state has no economic way of determining what to do, how to do it, or how much to do it. And it is invasive because it will necessarily aggressively interfere with people and their property. Thus even when there are some clear gainers as a result of an intervention, politics is always a negative-sum system that is destructive of wealth and liberty.

Let us briefly contrast liberty with politics in some general categories.

Education

Before the start of major state involvement in education, in 1870, basic literacy in the UK was already over 90%. Today, depending on the source, somewhere between 20% and 50% of school leavers are reported to be functionally illiterate. At the same time, the state manipulates examination results to pretend that educational standards are always rising. And the state's attempt to increase paper qualifications of all kinds adds bureaucratic waste. Educational standards will only rise again if the state gets out of the way at all levels. That said, a lot of education is mainly a consumer good that is wrongly presented as investment in human capital.

Physical infrastructure

'Physical infrastructure' means the things that are needed to connect individual homes and businesses. It includes such things as roads, railways, water and sewage, power supplies and telephone lines. People sometimes assert that the market either cannot provide these things efficiently or that it cannot provide them at all. But increasingly these are accepted as all being capable of efficient private production. When roads, for instance, are private (as they sometimes are now and were in the past) then tolls can ensure that only the users pay for them. And today, electronic charging and varying the price can minimise traffic congestion. For many years the lighthouse was held to be the archetypal, non-excludable, public good that the state had to produce. But we now know that even lighthouses were often provided privately, though always hampered by state 'assistance' that crowds out private alternatives.

Healthcare

Whether or not it is a sign of medical progress, it is significant that there were more hospital beds in the UK before the start of the National Health Service in 1948 than the NHS has beds today. And they did not have two administrators for each bed. The NHS is a bottomless pit of waste and poor healthcare that becomes worse the more tax-money it receives. A move towards full private insurance would greatly improve healthcare. Also, the state regulation of medical qualifications and drugs is a barrier to competition that further lowers health standards.

Welfare payments

Before the state implemented so-called National Insurance funded by compulsory "contributions" (in effect a tax on jobs), people were already opting for a variety of genuine welfare-insurance schemes. The state crowded out those private schemes with its own wasteful version. We should return to the voluntary schemes. The tiny percentage of people who would have no insurance or savings and are perceived to be in genuine need would be far better helped by charity.

Victimless crimes

States often pick on some voluntary or consensual activities and declare them to be 'crimes'. The major example of our time is recreational drug use. We are told that people suffer ill health and even die from using certain drugs. There are also the harmful effects on others of drug-user crime and gangsterism. A typical libertarian reply is to argue that usage dangers are grossly exaggerated. Drinking alcohol, smoking tobacco, and other legal activities, such as some sports, are statistically more damaging to health. Many long-term, illegal-drug users remain in as good health as comparable non-users. To the extent that they do not, this is partly because of the unreliable quality of the drugs caused by the illegality itself. The illegality also reduces the supply of the drugs and so raises their price. And this is what prompts some users to commit crimes to pay for them and attracts sellers who can only operate outside state law.

Social justice

If 'social justice' means not having damaging and unnecessary social differences in society, then only liberty approaches giving us this. For instance, the modern state often uses aggressive coercion to 1) impose some degree of material equality, and 2) prohibit discrimination with respect to a person's race, sex, etc. But the free market promotes both of these insofar as they are economic. 1) Over time, competition causes differences in income and profit to be reduced. Any remaining differences are necessary to reward the greater productivity that still exists. 2) Businesses do not discriminate on an arbitrary basis concerning employees or customers, or they would be out-competed by businesses that do not. Imposing greater equality and non-discrimination than liberty allows is both unjust and inefficient.

The real class conflict

People sometimes complain that the 'class system' is unjust (possibly conflating it with the, predominantly, caste system of aristocracy). But insofar as individuals and families can achieve varying degrees of socio-economic success according to their own efforts under conditions of free competition, such meritocratic 'class' is what encourages people to be socially productive. However, there is a genuine problem of class conflict. There is the class of those people who are (net) tax-receivers. They live off the class of those people who are (net) taxpayers. The tax-receiving, or tax-parasitic, class needs to be abolished so that those people find productive jobs in the free market.

Law and order

Common law that protects people and their property originally evolved without the state. State legislation typically flouts that law and thereby the liberty it preserves. And if we include all the security guards, store detectives, night watchmen, doormen, and so forth, then state police have always been a minority of overall policing. But state police are a very expensive and inefficient tax-parasitic minority that aggress against liberty more than they protect it. A move towards depoliticised law and full private policing would give us the law and order that we largely lack today.

National defence

'National defence' means defending the population of a country (the nation). This rarely, if ever, happens. At best, political 'national defence' is more about defending an existing state from a competing state that is hardly any worse, if worse at all, and certainly not worth the death and destruction caused by defending it. But many wars are aggressive attacks on other countries on one pretext or other. The result is invariably vastly more death and destruction than if the attacks had not taken place. This not only applies to recent invasions of other countries but even more so to becoming unnecessarily involved in conflicts leading up to and including World Wars I and II. A voluntarily funded national defence would stick to real defence. And as we have seen in Vietnam and, repeatedly, in Afghanistan, a country with polycentric and grassroots resistance can be impossible to conquer and rule.

Tacit consent to politics?

Do we tacitly consent to taxes and legislation by living in a country and participating in democracy? And by this consent is politics libertarian after all? No. We do not consent to crime just because we live in an area where crime is known to exist. Nor do we consent to crime if we find a way of recovering some of the value of what was stolen from us. We do not, in fact, have democracy but elected oligarchy. If we attempt to minimise any damage that our rulers do by voting for the least bad candidate, then that is not to consent to the damage the state causes. The state does rest on majority acceptance that it is needed. But this popular error cannot make state aggression either libertarian or legitimate.

The way forward

If all this is true, then the state is really a giant criminal organisation. Its taxation is extortion and its legislation is authoritarianism. But if we can persuade enough people to see that liberty is the most important social value and that politics is liberty's greatest enemy, then eventually the state can be rolled back. It is true that there has never been a large society without a state. There has never been one without disease either. But both politics and disease are evils that ought to be resisted and reduced as far as possible.

2) My Greatest Fear: the State

(A short talk given at one of Christian Michel's intellectual *soirées*, 2006.)

My greatest fear is quite predictable once you know that I am a libertarian. It is far more obvious and alarming to me than would be the clichéd "elephant in the living room" (a dangerous but only temporary nuisance and fairly rare in central London). It is the leviathan (the state) in the entire country (indeed, at least one in every country). In England it is now partly the UK-state and partly the Euro-state.

Look at what the state does all the time. It takes away many of our rights to do what we like with our persons and property. And it increasingly takes away more of those rights. It is perverse to fear being robbed when every single week the state takes somewhere between a quarter and a half of our incomes. And that is before taxes on the products you buy. Plus the state often extorts further amounts on an opportunistic crime basis, such as at least one hundred billion pounds stolen from private pension funds by 'prudent' Gordon Brown (who is more like a one-eyed Scotch pirate). And there is also the never-ending monetary inflation that is tantamount to counterfeiting: M4 has accelerated to 14.4% for the year since October 2005.[1] Price-inflation is always cited by the state because that is lessened by increased production; but discussing only price-inflation is like discussing only the visible part of an iceberg.

The main pretext for the modern state's interventions is to guarantee the provision of essential services. What about education? Objective literacy and numeracy rates continue to decline despite claims that examination results are improving year after year. Or the National-Socialist Health Service? A bottomless pit of inefficiency that absorbs ever larger sums of tax-extorted resources yet provides fewer hospital beds than before the NHS began; with growing waiting lists for treatment and an ever-expanding bureaucracy. Or pensions? Far lower than they would have been had the 'National Insurance' money be invested in the private economy (and insured) instead of a pay-as-you-go scheme that uses current taxes to finance pensions for those already retired. Or non-state crime? Rising over time thanks to the hopeless state-police monopoly.[2]

The state also uses our resources for a never-ending succession of foreign military adventures. These are always pictured as noble crusades but invariably result in more deaths and destruction than would ever have occurred otherwise (including the entry into both world wars). In Iraq the current figures from the latest Lancet article[3] estimate over 650,000 additional deaths due to the invasion (and all this has been a major cause of both an actual terrorist attack and many other alleged terrorist plots within the UK); while the opportunity cost to the USA alone has been estimated at three trillion dollars. All non-state criminal activity combined cannot begin to approach the amount of death, theft and destruction that people tolerate from the state.

Consider what might have occurred if there had not been a state for, say, only the last fifty years. The British state consumes about half of all that is produced each year—year after year. The compound damage this does is to slow all scientific, technological, economic and moral progress to a tiny fraction of what it could and ought to be. Many, possibly all, types of cancer might have been cured by now and possibly even ageing (by stem cell research or some other way as yet unguessed by us). Poverty might still exist as a matter of definition, as it is a relative concept. But the standard of living of the poorest quintile would substantially overlap with that of the richest quintile today. So poverty would not be a real problem. Indeed, tolerating market inequality is the solution to any real problems of poverty.

Most people do not fear the state—in fact, they love it. They are convinced that the state provides a solution to all the problems that, in truth, its very existence causes. The state has an inherently aggressive and predatory relationship with its subjects, and enables its subjects to prey on each other through tax-extorted subventions and oppressive legislation passing for just law. This all amounts to what is known in game theory as a negative sum game. By contrast, the relationships among the members of a free society exemplify mutual aid and amount to a positive sum game. Carl von Clausewitz said, "War is the continuation of politics by other means." We can reverse this and see that politics is the continuation of war by other means. But most people can't see it. People have to be taught to fear the state as destructive and stupid. For the state rests on their support. When their support eventually evaporates and turns to antipathy, as it will, the state will fall. Only then will the political nightmare end and full civilisation finally begin.

Notes

[1] For the latest data see
http://www.bankofengland.co.uk/statistics/ms/current/index.htm
and
http://www.bankofengland.co.uk/statistics/ms/2006/oct/taba2.1.2.xls.

[2] Those who think that a state must evolve from any attempt at private protection agencies should read Murray Rothbard's "Robert Nozick and the immaculate conception of the state."
[3] www.thelancet.com/webfiles/images/journals/lancet/s0140673606694919.pdf

3) The Good, the Bad, and the Neutral: Abortion

(In lieu of a lost article on abortion: 1979 meets 2009.)

In 1979, in my first term of my first philosophy degree, I decided that I had definitively solved the philosophical problems surrounding abortion, unlike any of the other philosophers on the relevant reading list. And so I duly submitted my essay on the issue to *Philosophy and Public Affairs*, and they duly rejected it. Although I did not fully realise it at the time, and did not become a libertarian for a few more years, it was a defence of abortion by way of one type of libertarian analysis. However, even self-identified libertarians strongly disagree about this controversial issue. And the consensus view of the feminist group I spoke to back then was that they would rather not have people like me on their side. I no longer have a copy of that essay but I remember the main points clearly enough. And those points have remained with me in a somewhat more sophisticated form some thirty years later. So for want of the essay itself, I will outline the gist of the arguments, without all the thought-experiments of the original, and then give the 2009 version of those arguments as they appear in my *A Libertarian Dictionary* (forthcoming).

The gist. If, other things being equal, killing someone is morally bad and saving someone from death is morally good, then presumably letting someone die must in itself be neutral. If it is not neutral, then, because there is an immensely large number people that we do let die (by not sending the world's poorest people all our income, for instance), we are all immensely bad when merely inactive—which is *prima facie* absurd. However, we also abstain from an immense amount of murder (it is not a difficult thing to kill someone) and that must, by parity of reasoning, in itself make us all immensely good when merely inactive—which is equally *prima facie* absurd in itself plus also logically absurd because contradictory when combined with our previous conclusion. Hence there must be moral room for neutrality, and that best fits abortion. Abortion is, in effect and in principle (and can be technically made to be in reality if required), letting die rather than killing. It is the withdrawing of an uncontractual benefit rather than the imposition of a cost. Moreover, the unborn human being is not a person in the intellectual sense but merely a potential person, just like any sperm and ovum that could be brought together. Doubtless, this is all far too brief to be completely clear and cogent for most people. Perhaps the following updated dictionary entries will help to elucidate these points (superscript asterisks indicate other dictionary entries).

abortion Abortion is *libertarian for two separate and cogent reasons, as well as being *utilitarian: 1) although a *person in the sense of being a member of our species, the unborn human is not a person in the *morally relevant sense of intellectual development; 2) the unborn human is not *proactively imposed on when the continuing gift of life-support is stopped.

1) The unborn human being, at whatever stage of development and given whatever technical label, is not a person in the intellectual-attainment sense—because not yet capable of *critical-theorising—that is necessary to give normal human beings their peculiar moral value. It is a potential person, but then so are any sperm and ovum that could be conjoined; or even any food that could eventually be converted into a person (the *Scholastics distinguished active potential, requiring action to stop it, from passive potential, requiring action to start it; but this appears to involve the ultimately incoherent *act-omission doctrine). If it is not inherently immoral to kill a non-person, as most *animals are, then it is not inherently immoral to kill an unborn human. Neither is it inherently immoral to kill an infant not yet a person, although there might be bad social side-effects of one kind or another (such as greatly upsetting some people who might also resort to violence); it is probably best to draw a line for infanticide, erring on the side of non-personhood, maybe sometime in the first year or two after birth and always well before speech indicates personhood. And the agreement of any parents or guardians would be necessary and sufficient, as they have *property *rights in the non-person.

It might be suggested, as a reductio, that by this standard an unconscious or comatose person is only a potential person, and so morally on a par with an unborn as regards killing him. But, as long as consciousness can be recovered, it looks far more reasonable to see this as a person whose consciousness is temporarily interrupted, and so full rights remain.

2) Even if an unborn human were a person in the intellectual sense, it would not be infringing his *liberty, or negative rights, to withdraw the uncontracted-for support of the womb so that he dies. This is merely to discontinue giving a gift. It might be suggested that, at least if it is a person, there is a (quasi-)*contract between the mother and the unborn human to bring him to term. But there is no kind of offer or acceptance of that offer (or any quid pro quo), which contracts require. There is only support started and then stopped. It is like starting and later stopping a bank order that *charitably supports someone in genuine *need; or

throwing a drowning man a rope but then not pulling him all the way to safety (*see* *act-omission doctrine). (However, to abandon one's child once he is a person, would be proactively to impose on him. This would be like offering someone a lift across the desert and then leaving him stranded in the middle of it. In each case we have actively put someone in harm's way. So we have a libertarian *duty to ensure his continued care in some way.)

As for utility, forcing women to bear unwanted *children cannot plausibly increase overall welfare compared to allowing them to bear children when they wish to do so.

People often deny either or both of 1 and 2. With 1, mistakenly asserting, or merely presupposing, that human beings cannot conceptually or practically be separated from personhood. With 2, mistakenly asserting, or merely presupposing, that there is some kind of contract to support the unborn that is created by its mother, and possibly its father too; or that to fail to support is here somehow equivalent to proactively killing (it does add to the confusion that abortions often take the form of destroying the unborn human in utero rather than removing it intact, but both are really methods of discontinuing support). People with a *religious background, are particularly prone to these errors. What they often also believe is that the unborn has a personal soul that has been called into existence or placed in the body, and for that reason the unborn cannot morally be killed or even have support withdrawn. In such cases, this underlying metaphysical belief is part of what has to be criticized.

If people feel strongly that abortion is murder, then they can choose to live in *private-property areas, or join any private *organization, where abortions are contractually proscribed on pain of whatever penalties they wish (including a no-opting-out clause if they want it: *see* *specific performance).

All that said, what we do to the unborn where they later go on to become persons can proactively impose in the same way that what we do to children can (*see* *age of consent; *circumcision, infibulation, etc. of children). Although the outcomes to the child be the same, there is a crucial causal and moral difference between *proactively imposing a *cost (which is unlibertarian) and merely withholding a benefit (which is libertarian); but which is which is less clear with an unborn because it is both dependent and a potential person.

On a related issue, where the man provides his sperm freely and without contract during sexual intercourse, he cannot have any libertarian rights concerning the unborn. And in the same way, a woman who freely chooses to risk unprotected or imperfectly protected sex without a contract does not have any rightful claims over the man if she becomes pregnant.

To gain any such rights a contract is required, such as a *marriage contract.

act-omission doctrine It is a matter of debate in *moral *philosophy, whether there is a real moral distinction between acting and failing to act when the outcome is the same. For instance, is there a difference between pushing someone into a river so that he drowns and failing to throw him a lifebelt so that he drowns? The act-omission doctrine is simply that there is a significant moral difference.

*Libertarians are often sympathetic to this distinction, and can see it as always permissible not to act in the sense that one is merely not getting involved. However, mere physical action and inaction cannot seem to capture the idea that libertarianism itself requires. One can, for instance, fail to act and thereby break a *contract, which cannot be libertarian. In whatever way the mere physical distinction is worded, it seems to fall foul of some such *criticism. There is, nevertheless, an *objective and moral distinction that is often detectable in many such examples: that between merely withholding a benefit and *proactively imposing a *cost. In fact, interpersonal *liberty can be theorised as the 'absence of proactively imposed costs'. This is a more abstract distinction than the physical act-omission one, though, and so more open to debatable interpretation.

person There is an important intellectual, and *moral, sense of being a person that, intuitively, is not conceptually linked with being a human being. A human being need not be a person (if a foetus or brain-dead, for instance) and a person need not be human (any sufficiently sophisticated conscious being would qualify). But what makes a person a person in this sense, and why does it matter?

Self-consciousness cannot in itself be a sufficient criterion, as is sometimes thought (oddly, it might not even be necessary; although consciousness or sentience is). *Animals probably have some degree of self-consciousness even at quite primitive levels: in order to distinguish between themselves and their environments for survival purposes. An aspect of *language usage appears to be more relevant. Many animals use language at the lower levels, to express emotions and to signal (sometimes dishonestly) and describe (even bees, in their way, describe directions to pollen by the 'dance' that they do in front of the other bees in the hive). Only human beings use language critically, or argumentatively, and theoretically. This *critical-theoretical, or meta-theoretical (in a sense, *philosophical), function of language enables typical human beings to rise above their immediate beliefs and desires and enter an intellectual realm that has a content that extends beyond their consciousness. If we consider the 'three worlds' of Karl Popper (1902-1994), loosely but mnemonically,

1) matter, 2) mind, 3) *memes (here meaning intellectual products of the mind as encoded in matter), then we can add the relevant and anterior realm 0) modes: the realm of all possible ideas (including *facts). Being able to enter this realm critically is an intellectual sense of being a 'person' and may be what distinguishes typical human beings from beasts. Being a person appears to involve simply achieving this critical-theoretical ability; which is not to imply that one ceases to be a person if temporarily unconscious (just as a scientist is still a scientist when not engaged in science). One does not become more of a person as one becomes better at this. Other things being equal, however, one's life might become more valuable to oneself.

Consider a chimpanzee that can talk in sign language, as some that have been taught by humans can do. If it could count objects up to ten, or say "walk" when it wanted a walk, or "food" when it wanted food, then we would be impressed but still consider it a sort of beast. But if it started to express and critically assess theories (as no chimpanzee has yet done), with testable and manifest understanding, then we should think of it as beyond a mere beast.

Being a person is so important that most persons would judge, along with J. S. Mill (1806-1873) that, "It is better to be a human being [i.e., a person] dissatisfied than a pig [i.e., a beast] satisfied". (Mill continues, "better to be Socrates [i.e., a philosopher] dissatisfied than a fool [or, presumably, any person of more limited intellectual faculties] satisfied. And if the fool, or the pig, are of a different opinion, it is because they only know their own side of the question. The other party to the comparison knows both sides." *Utilitarianism*, 1863.) The state of being a person is thus qualitatively different from being a beast. Persons have more intrinsic *value than beasts, just as beasts have more intrinsic value than plants (which is not to say greater value in all possible circumstances). And there are things that it is permissible to do to the latter but not to the former in each case. Thus mere hedonistic *utilitarianism is refuted. Therefore, *libertarianism is not arbitrary in focusing on *liberty for persons, rather than beasts. And persons can defensibly value the liberty to err more highly than *paternalism that aims at making them more hedonistically satisfied, even if that paternalism could be guaranteed to be incorrupt and efficient at achieving its goals (both of which are highly unlikely).

It is clearly possible to have theories without putting them into language (symbolic representation). Most daily thoughts are non-linguistic: experiences and inclinations, etc. Language is mainly used as a mnemonic for oneself and to communicate with others. But it is not clear that it is possible to enter the critical-theoretical realm of personhood without language. Would telepathic persons, *qua* persons, think in linguistic symbols or only images? This theoretical sketch of intellectual personhood need not attempt an answer.

4) Murder, and Child and Animal Abuse

(A reply to Sean Fox in *Free Life*, vol. 4, no. 2, 1983.)

There is no settled libertarian position on any of the issues raised by Sean Fox[1] The treatment of children and animals is an especially contentious area. Rothbard is not the first or last word on libertarianism and neither am I. I am an anarcho-capitalist—like Rothbard—whilst many libertarians are minimal statists, but I don't have much time for talk of natural rights—unlike Rothbard and many others. I am a libertarian out of a combination of a certain amount of natural human benevolence and a considerable amount of sheer self-interest. I think people, including myself, become better off (by their own standards) the freer that society becomes. And I like the idea of this happening.

Libertarian law would primarily protect the individual from force (this includes theft) and fraud. On this I think we can all agree. Such aspects of common law existed prior to statutory law and will persist after it. These will be found in any advanced society for they are a necessary prop to civilisation. Discussing the likely types of law seems quite useful, but, as I said, within the framework of anarcho-capitalism *sans* natural rights. Though precisely which laws would evolve in a free market is impossible to say.

The murderer and his victim

Such laws might well protect the individual's interests after his death, rather as they might were he merely unconscious or comatose. Ensuring that his last will and testament is adhered to rather than allowing his property to be seized would be an example of such protection.

It is obvious that a dead man cannot act. What happens after a man's death can still be the result of his action and he can be held responsible for it. A dying man might plant a time-bomb to kill a particular innocent person after his own death (maybe years later). He would only become a murderer when the bomb goes off and kills his victim. Similarly, someone can initiate a legal arrangement that would continue after his death. It would be the result of his action and he would be responsible for it. So the murder victim can already have taken appropriate action by insuring himself. His probable motive for taking such action would primarily be deterrence. The insurance company would prosecute on behalf of its murdered client as arranged. Not to do so would be tantamount to accepting that their clients could be murdered with impunity. This might be bad for business.

But why does the murder victim have to initiate the action for it to be legitimate? (When I use 'legitimate' I generally mean 'compatible with libertarianism'.) Charity is absolutely legitimate. Acting without payment on someone else's behalf to protect his interests from coercion is an act of charity. It seems legitimate to act in someone's interests either when he is alive and cannot protect himself or when he has been murdered. (For a person's interests can continue after his death as can the consequences of his actions. That people make wills is an example of this.)

One does not need this motive legitimately to ensure that the murderer is taken care of. People will pay out of their own interests to see that murderers do not roam the streets—they might be the next terrorist victims. Pre-emptive measures for self-defence need not be anti-libertarian.

The murderer would recompense the beneficiaries of the victim's will. Otherwise his family and maybe his friends or even his favourite charity could normally receive payment (via the insurance company, lawyers, or the courts). Legal action is not merely for extracting restitution but also to punish. Restitution is important and much neglected by the state but it is certainly not the only legitimate function of legal redress. People usually want punishments that will act as deterrents first and only restitution, and possibly retribution, afterwards. The kind of punishment that is appropriate is best determined by the market. What the murderer receives will be what people are prepared to pay to see that the punishment deters other potential murderers and satisfies their moral outrage.

The idea that revenge (or retribution) has a place in law is, perhaps, controversial. If people demand extreme punishments as the price for certain crimes that they regard as especially awful, then that is as much up to them as setting a price for any goods they possess. If the would-be murderer, or whatever, wants to avoid paying the price he has only to avoid the crime in question. I accept the free-market solution because I expect people to pay a lot to avoid coercion and thus cut down the number of murderers, whilst I expect no effective demand to stop victimless 'crimes' (such as watching 'nasty' videos).

If someone cannot or does not insure himself against murder, and he is murdered, and no one is prepared to catch the culprit, then I am not convinced that the murderer remaining unpunished would always "clearly be unsatisfactory". (We may seem to have this situation when we 'murder' other animals.) If people don't want to pay for this service are they to be taxed? If they prefer to take a risk if there is one, then let them.

One can also reject the assumption that libertarian principles preclude the possibility that one can have property rights (in a legitimate legal sense) over another's body. All contracts of employment cede some measure of property rights over oneself. Why shouldn't I sign a contract to sell a kidney? The extreme case is selling oneself into slavery. Inalienable natural rights lead to a traditional paradox here: if you can sell your freedom, then your rights aren't inalienable; if you can't, then your personal freedom isn't complete. I can see no reason that slavery is necessarily incompatible with libertarianism. The freedom to end one's freedom by slavery seems just as much a necessary part of full personal freedom as is the freedom to end one's freedom by suicide. (Suicide would almost always be a much more drastic personal decision.) I don't think selling oneself into slavery will ever really catch on though. It would be as absurd to think slavery might become popular as it would be to think that *hara-kiri* might. Libertarianism only allows these possibilities. It does not follow that they will become acceptable and I certainly don't condone them.

Infanticide and child abuse

Murder is culpable killing. I do not think that killing a child that is totally dependent or parasitic on oneself is culpable any more than is abortion or 'wasting' sperm and ova. Paradoxically, perhaps, I do find objectionable the idea of leaving the infant to die of starvation or exposure—but only because of the suffering that results. If we decide to withdraw our support then this is not an act of force or fraud. Having decided not to support the 'parasite'—maybe because it is deformed—if it is on our property and we don't wish that another should take it, then euthanasia would seem preferable—even a moral obligation—to being responsible for unnecessary suffering. This is common practice, I understand, in NHS hospitals (using injections). One is not aiming at death here, for that would come anyway without continued support.

In Britain mothers who do not want their children rarely abandon them in the street, let alone kill them. There is no reason to suppose that people would be more cold-hearted in a free society. Individual conscience and social disapproval would continue to be enough to prevent such things increasing. Adoption and fostering would remain popular alternatives. In fact, statism positively encourages a 'the government should do something' attitude, which prevents such things becoming even more common.

Actual torture of innocent children is as anti-libertarian as torture of innocent adults. A libertarian society would not tolerate it if it were detected. People might pay to see that any child is protected from violence. It is no problem that it may be necessary to go on a criminal's property to prevent such acts. Infringing malefactors' normal liberties is necessary if there is to be any law and order. But forcing all parents to allow regular child inspectors into their homes just because abuse is a possibility, could only do more harm than good. We have to accept that some child abuse will, as with murder, always exist.

On the reasonable assumption that children are not likely to be imprisoned by their parents, they could also protect themselves. At two years old, or so, the maltreated child may flee to the sanctuary of a neighbour or even a passer-by. Most people would help a child in distress. I doubt that a protection agency would want to be seen returning a child to parents who abuse it. Unlike now, the final say as to whom to stay with would be the child's.

Abuse of animals

I expect animals to be treated largely as property. I think many animal rightists anthropomorphise them considerably but I accept that many animals can feel intense physical and psychological pain and discomfort. I don't think animals have natural rights but then I don't think people do either—if these entail an 'objective' (independently existing, single, true) morality.

Like most human beings, I find the torture of animals repugnant; I also find animals very tasty (though I once went for three years without eating anybody). I do not like the rhetoric about us being persons whilst they are mere beasts and so absolutely, qualitatively, different. There is an obvious continuum between the lowest animals and ourselves. To make such a distinction may make some people feel happier but I believe it is dishonest. I think it preferable to admit that we have enslaved these sentient creatures for our own pleasures. However, if we didn't like various animal products there would probably be considerably fewer of those animals anyway. And most other animals can't suffer the expectation of their eventual 'murder' and the indignity of 'slavery' as we could. And most (of the tasty ones, at least) do not suffer if they lose a 'spouse' or 'friend'.

Gratuitous animal suffering is best tackled by consumer sovereignty. As people grow wealthier (thanks to free-market industrialisation) they tend to become more humane and outward-looking. Consumer agencies that report cruelties will be increasingly in demand—they already exist—and offending companies will be boycotted. This happens now over cosmetics, amongst other products. The companies themselves have begun to realise the value of such slogans as 'beauty without pain'.

The effect will increase, the more that people realise that they cannot pass the buck to the state on such issues. Not that the state has ever done much to prevent cruelty to animals; far from it in many cases. The disgusting LD5O test (where the Lethal Dose of some substance is continued until 50% of the animals involved are dead) is used all the time. Yet the companies know that it is often useless and they would rather be testing reasonable doses on willing human subjects (many of whom might be terminally ill anyway) if only it were legal. The government also finances much useless animal experimentation in universities, defence establishments, etc.

I have not attempted to make sense of limited statist or natural rightist approaches because I could not really say to what conclusions such ideas are supposed to lead or why.

Note

[1] For Sean Fox's letter see *Free Life*, vol. 4, no. 2, Libertarian Alliance online.

5) The Pure Joy of Heroin

(*Free Life*, vol.4, no. 2, 1985.)

The media's latest spate of heroin-bashing started, as far as I can tell, with a piece in *Time Out* (March 1984). What is remarkable about this report is that the evidence for the supposed harmful effects of the drug is almost entirely absent—there were no deaths or even accidents on the South London estates investigated—despite the obviously disapproving tone of the reporter. Since then the evidence against heroin has become less and less alarming in proportion as the rhetoric of the media has become more and more hysterical.

However, truth and good sense will out; if not from the reporters and leader writers of the popular press then from informed people in their journals (such is the virtue of free speech). In the *Daily Star* and *The Daily Mirror,* Mrs Jackson, wife of the actor Gordon Jackson, told us of her son who had kicked his heroin habit: "I can't see what all the fuss is about. My son was just having some fun. It's the fashion these days." As if to emphasize this no-nonsense approach, Pinklon Thomas won the World Boxing Council heavyweight title—six years after ending his heroin use. Thomas had enjoyed heroin for seven years, from the age of thirteen to twenty, before he decided to box. He achieved a strapping 15 stone six pounds to fight with. By the time of his title he had notched up 25 wins, no defeats, one draw and 21 knockouts! Anecdotal evidence though this may seem, it certainly knocks out the theory about heroin users being on a fast and certain road to death. Eventually two doctors, independently of each other, baldly admitted (in *The Sunday Times* and *The Observer*) that they knew of no evidence that heroin causes bodily or mental damage. This observation was repeated by the only General Practitioner allowed to prescribe the drug, and who has customers of a couple of decades' standing (*Newsnight*, BBC TV, 30th January 1985). Heroin is not a poison and that is that.

Although the moral right to take risks with one's own life and even certainly to damage oneself is the key issue, it is still worth clearing up a few empirical matters. Heroin is not a disease, it is simply a habit. Heroin users start and stop by choice. If one wants to emphasise that it can be physically addictive, then one should remember that many addictions are enjoyable and often even widely approved of: tea, chocolate, sport (the chemical effects on the brain of regular vigorous exercise are similar to the effects of taking opiates).

DHSS reassurance

It is true that all physical addictions have withdrawal symptoms; that is what being addicted means. As the dear ladies of the *Good Housekeeping Family Health Encyclopaedia* tell us:

> Opiates bind to special receptors on the surface of the nerve cells in the parts of the brain and the spinal cord dealing with the processing of information about pain. These receptors interact with enkephalins, chemicals manufactured by the brain which are released when pain impulses pass along the spinal cord to help suppress the sensation of pain before it becomes intolerable ... opiates taken habitually ... gradually cause production of enkephalins to cease. If the supply of opiates is cut off, pain returns, since there are no enkephalins left to deal with it. The body craves for more opiates as a result and withdrawal symptoms make their appearance. (p. 103)

However, it is now widely reported that heroin withdrawal symptoms in most cases are no worse than flu or a bad cold:

> After several weeks on high doses sudden withdrawal results in a variable degree of discomfort generally comparable to a bout of influenza. (DHSS information booklet *Drug Misuse*, ISDD 1985.)

Even this is rare for most users. It has been shown by placebo tests that some users believe that they are addicted when they are not, and—it was claimed on *Diverse Reports* (Channel 4, 26 Sept. 1984)—only one in seven US users are addicted.

It is clear that the main reason that people continue this habit is not avoidance of withdrawal symptoms but desire for the bliss of the drug. Toleration cannot fully negate the pleasure. In recognition of this the latest anti-heroin drug 'cure', *Naltrexone*, is specifically designed to block the euphoria that heroin causes. It is admitted that this killjoy won't stop addiction unless the user decides to stop. Yet the possibility of giving up at any time one chooses already exists, as is well evidenced by the case of US soldiers in Vietnam: 70% of them used the drug when at war while very few used it when they returned home and had better things to do. The carnage of war left a mark on many of the men—not heroin. (It is quite possible that this self-prescribed medicine did a lot to protect them from the horror of war.)

Another myth is that regular heroin-users have to end as down-and-outs. There are many professional people who take drugs and still do their jobs properly. In the case of heroin one of the most interesting examples is that of doctors in the US who prefer heroin to golf when they want to relax. It seems they not only do their jobs but keep up with technical reading and generally function no differently from other physicians (see Walter Block's *Defending The Undefendable*, Fleet Press, p. 48). Judging the effects of heroin by the living conditions of the worst cases is like judging alcohol by the alcoholics who choose to live rough.

The only problem with heroin is that it is illegal. This has several bad consequences usually attributed to the drug itself. Prohibition causes a scarcity that keeps the price far higher than it would otherwise be. If it were allowed to be manufactured plentifully it would cost a small fraction of its present price. There would be no need to steal to pay for the habit if that habit were legal. Impairment of quality occurs because scarce heroin is adulterated, by dealers who cannot be sued for this practice, to get a better price; if easily available and legal this would be as likely as the adulteration of aspirin. Legality would prevent sickness caused by the presence of impurities and the deaths caused by overdosing due to an unexpectedly pure batch (for one can overdose on heroin as one can overdose on almost anything one ingests—such as aspirin, salt or even water; similarly heroin can be dangerous in combination with other chemicals as is common with many accepted drugs). The dirty needles that cause hepatitis—the most common cause of death among users—would be replaced by easily available supplies of clean ones.

> ... Laws can increase certain risks for those who do take them—risks of adulteration, uncertain purity, poor hygiene, high costs, inadequate or misleading information (p. 9) ... The physiological effects of long-term opiate use are rarely serious in themselves. But physical damage, associated largely with repeated, often unhygienic injecting, and with the injection of adulterants, is common amongst addicts (p. 12, *Drug Misuse*, ISDD, 1985).

Also, if legal, the innocent buyers and sellers of the good would no longer be harassed, arrested and imprisoned. And the hapless public wouldn't be forced to pay for this vicious anti-social behaviour.

But even if the heroin habit were as risky as Russian roulette—so what? Should taking such risks be illegal? What about the risks involved in smoking, eating fatty foods, not taking regular exercise, sexual intercourse, or crossing the road? (As all people take avoidable risks, all deaths—except completely unforeseen ones—might be viewed as forms of suicide.) Why point at some level of risk-taking a little higher than our own and say that it should not be allowed? One reason that people do it is simply intolerance of different ways of life. Another reason in this case is the cultural prejudice against certain chemicals even though other pastimes, such as hang-gliding, might be demonstrably far more dangerous. There are no good moral reasons. These things are partially caused and reinforced by the law. Intolerant prejudice against this innocent pleasure would fade if state witch hunts stopped. In the free market people learn that it is cheaper to tolerate the personal behaviour of others.

All these problems can be cured by legalisation, but there is another suggestion that is becoming increasingly popular: nationalising the heroin industry. *The Observer* (2 Sept., 1984) tells us that the Amsterdam City Council, "is developing an alternative, based on the insight that the drug is not itself harmful to the bodies and minds of those who use it ... its dangers stem directly from its illegality ... ", so they are supplying users "with a legal source to remove them from the black market's dangers." This is not enough for the *Junkiebund* (the junkies' union) who want it available free from their own doctors.

This is not a new idea. In the *New Statesman* (4 Jan., 1985) the reporter suggests the possibility that the dominance of the illicit market and the present uncontrolled situation might have been avoided if the British government had continued with the policy of the 1950s and 60s when heroin was manufactured legally and prescribed by doctors. He suggests a debate about a return to this system. Similar suggestions were made by the editor of the *New Statesman* in *The Times* (5 Feb., 1985) and on Channel 4's *Diverse Reports* (26 Sept., 1984). But it seems that it was fashion that caused heroin to spread in the 1960s and it is fashion and low prices that are causing it to spread even more rapidly in the 1980s. Heroin on the NHS is not the solution to the problems caused by its illegality—legalising heroin is the only solution; not merely a little more of the good stuff available at public expense, but plenty of the good stuff manufactured for profit in a legitimate industry. The present anti-heroin legislation is a menace to health as well as depriving us of liberty.

Many drugs are a great pleasure and solace in life. Contra the pristine utilitarians, pleasure is only one of the things that humans value, though it is an important one. Nobody wants to be entirely without pleasure, but nobody wants to devote their lives to pleasure exclusively—certainly not the average heroin-user: they have friendships, hobbies and ambitions like the rest of us. If the use of certain drugs, or any activity, is likely to risk shortening life or damaging us, then the individual is best placed to decide how much risk or damage is worth paying. In this case, one would do well to remember that a life without any pleasurable drugs would not generally be that much longer or safer—but it certainly might seem a lot longer.

6) The Ulster Nation: Troops Out, Market In

(With David McDonagh from *Free Life*, vol. 4, no. 3, 1985.)

Is Mrs Thatcher really a "traitor"? The answer must be "yes" because the Anglo-Irish Agreement surrenders some UK sovereignty, which is a treacherous act. But such treachery is not wrong in itself. The nation-state must eventually be dismantled if people perceive the superiority of market-anarchy. What is wrong with this agreement is that Mrs Thatcher has taken steps to allow some relatively enlightened and free thinking people in the UK to come under the control of a relatively barbarous, intolerant, theocratic state. The religious nature of the state is only objectionable because religions should be voluntary affairs. That it is an alien state is not relevant (except in so far as this reduces Republican Nationalists' claims to absurdity), for if it were a more liberal alien state then this Agreement might be desirable.

That the Anglo-Irish Agreement must be viewed as an illiberal move is incontrovertibly illustrated by the nature and constitution of the foreign power that Parliament (for Mrs Thatcher is not alone in her treachery) has allowed to have a say in the governing of Ulster.

Expansionist republican theocracy

The state in the south of Ireland was established largely by staunch Roman Catholics. As a result it has developed into a theocracy, with comprehensive Catholicisation beginning in 1923 by common consent. The 1937 constitution had written into it that legislation must be grounded in Catholic theology. Political leaders in Eire must defer to the Church of Rome on all important social issues. When in doubt on any such issue the government calls on the bishops for their advice. As a result we find abortion is unconstitutional as well as illegal. Contraception is limited. There is no right to divorce. The Supreme Court has declared that a man's wife is his chattel. Homosexuals are gaoled.

The second and third articles of Eire's constitution spell out their position on the North unambiguously:

> 2) The national territory consists of the whole island of Ireland, its islands and the territorial seas.

3) Pending the reintegration of the national territory, and without prejudice to the right of the Parliament and Government established by this Constitution to exercise jurisdiction over the whole of that territory, the laws enacted by that Parliament shall have the like area and extent of application as the laws of Saorstal Eireann [Irish Free State] and the like extra-territorial effect.

Republican foothold

So the Southern Irish Government's "recognition" of Ulster as part of the UK is bogus. In the Agreement they were allowed to strike out the reference to Northern Ireland "as part of the United Kingdom", and were therefore happy to acknowledge merely "no change in the status of Northern Ireland"! The constitution invalidates any concessionary interpretation of the Agreement as the Republic's government and population are very well aware. With their right to criticise the North and a guarantee of British attempts to meet these criticisms they have a foothold. The price, the Republic's "guarantee" to co-operate over terrorists, existed before this Agreement so it costs them nothing. Their press has written about this Agreement as meaning virtual joint sovereignty with long-term leverage to swallow Ulster. They are jubilant.

The two Irish nations in context

In 1800 Ireland had the makings of a single Protestant, Whig nation. In that year the Act of Union ended a rebellion that in France and America had set up new regimes bent on becoming modern states. Ireland got linked to the 1689 modern British state (that was born of the Glorious Revolution of 1688) and so Whigs in Ireland, as in England, ceased to be revolutionary and became mere reformers. The Act of Union ended the Anglo-Irish as rulers. (Their chamber was as old as the one at Westminster but it was corrupt and so opposed by the Whigs.)

Yet between 1800 and 1830 a new and second nation arose on the island of Ireland. In Britain there were three nations: Wales, Scotland and England; in Ireland where there had been only one, there now emerged a second: Eire. Eire was a new nation, being a new separate society in the southern part of the island of Ireland. (That the two nations of Ireland do not officially have different names and that people use "Ireland' to cover both, is part of the problem. "Ireland" covers two nations, like "Britain" covers three. "Eire" is an ancient name, for the whole island of Ireland, that was appropriated by the new nation in the south who then claimed to represent the whole of Ireland. But calling the new southern nation "Eire" and the old northern nation "Ulster", as we do in this article, makes more sense.)

How Eire was born

Daniel O'Connell more than most men deserves the title of "father of his country". He was called to the Irish Bar in 1797 and later took up, as a Whig, the liberal cause of Catholic Emancipation (to free Catholic entry into both Parliament and university posts). O'Connell held Monster Meetings attended by many thousands of Gaels. His Catholic Association was strongly supported by priests and collected over £1,000 weekly. On being elected for County Clare in 1828, the House of Commons reformed the law to let him take his place in 1829. This cause had enjoyed the full support of the Whigs in the north, who did not yet see themselves as a separate nation. It was only when O'Connell went for the repeal of the Union that they began to see that Home Rule would mean Rome Rule.

At the Monster Meetings a remarkable sea change had occurred. The Gaels who went to the meetings had picked up English from translators of O'Connell's speeches. The Church had long since been keen to spread the use of English, but it failed until this new movement for Catholic Emancipation. The Gaels of the 18th century and beforehand were only nominal Catholics. Now they became very enthusiastic. Catholic Ireland was to become a source of Catholic missionaries for what they, with unintentional irony, held to be their 'old' religion. They were to go all over the world, from South America to China, to spread the 'old' faith (this shows the sort of energy the new nation commanded). In fact their Catholicism was as fresh as their English.

Sir Robert Peel became Prime Minister in 1841 and, as a former secretary of Ireland, set out to counter O'Connell's. attempt to repeal the Union. He had O'Connell arrested and made him cancel a Grand Monster Meeting at Clontarf in 1843. O'Connell was never quite the same force again and he died in 1847. But he left behind a new nation, and the modern Irish question. (And Whiggism, the ancestor of libertarianism, was left with a bad name in the South, which it retains to this day.)

The Irish question

What is the Irish Question? It is: "Can the new Irish nation, Eire, rule the whole island of Ireland?" The answer to it is: "No, because it does not have the power to conquer the older nation in Ulster, any more than Wales has the power to conquer Scotland." (In fact, the Scots came from what we now call Ireland in the 5th century.)

The present "troubles" are in considerable part the result of the 1920 Government of Ireland Act. Here Lloyd George deliberately set up a devolved Ulster to distance Ulster from the rest of the UK, in the hope that it would eventually leave and join the South. This gave the Irish Nationalists encouragement. The Protestants opposed this special treatment. It was, after all, the Home Rule that they had opposed (though now it no longer meant Rome Rule). The pristine Unionist aim in 1920 was to continue direct rule from Westminster. They expressed no wish to dominate the Catholics and predicted trouble; trouble that they wished to avoid by full UK membership. In Ulster they rubber-stamped Westminster legislation in a deliberate attempt to minimise the distancing which Lloyd George had created. The process of keeping Ulster at a distance has continued, though it has more recently taken the form of the refusal of the major political parties to organise in Ulster. Consequently normal politics is impossible, and each election is effectively a referendum on the Union.

The IRA-Sinn Fein

The Provisional IRA is not officially connected to or supported by the government of the Irish Republic, although the IRA shares their ambitions as regards the North. (This reminds us of the policy of Elizabeth the First towards Catholic Spain. Privately she encouraged Drake, Hawkins and company to plunder for the British crown and in the Protestant cause. But openly she denounced them as buccaneers and outlaws. She imprisoned and even executed many of them, declaring that her aim was to round up the rest.) Sinn Fein is the political wing of the IRA that operates with them in the North to establish, by the ballot box and the gun, Roman Catholic Nationalism on the whole of the island of Ireland. Sinn Fein made socialist noises in the 1930s and 1960s, and have done so again since 1982, but this seems to have been to gull socialists, their main supporters, on the British mainland. They intrigued with Nazi Germany in the early 1940s; in the 1950s and 1970s they championed a Catholic corporate state and Cold War struggle against atheistic communism. Sinn Fein-IRA's primary aim is, nevertheless, theocratic Irish nationalism.

It is hard to see how, as Enoch Powell suggested, American influence upon Mrs Thatcher can have suddenly caused her to do another of her famous U-turns; this time on her "forever British" stance on Ulster (her rigid rhetoric but plastic policies are more generally evidenced by her increased spending on state welfare and warfare combined with increased taxation). It seems more likely that it was the IRA who saw sense at last when they realised that bombing innocent people did not greatly worry politicians, who are used to treating other citizens as cannon fodder. The IRA sensibly killed Airey Neave (Thatcher's aide and mentor) before he could implement his policies for getting Ulster into normal UK politics. The Brighton bombing, seen from the IRA's point of view, was also very sensible for it must have left Mrs Thatcher badly shaken and fearing for her own life.

Who are the imperialists?

But having been bombed into submission, did Mrs Thatcher really need to try to throw Ulster to the South? Would it not have been better simply to give the terrorists what they say they want—"troops out". (What they really mean is "UK troops out", emasculating Ulster's indigenous defences in the process, and then Republican troops in.) With British troops gone the nationalists would lose their most important "anti-imperialist" argument and stand revealed as the would-be imperialists that they really are.

Imperialism need not be a disaster. It depends on the options. Free trade (i.e., anarchy) is better, but that's not on offer owing to lack of public demand. But different nationalist movements go in for different degrees of state control. And very often the new nationalist regimes around the world have proven to be even more reactionary than the empire was rather than more progressive; they have often led to a decline in living standards for the people in return for mere nominal freedoms. In contrast, through the cultural exchange and free trade that went with the Roman Empire, relative enlightenment and stability was brought to many areas over hundreds of years. Britain has no such liberalising effect on Ulster, though, for the Ulster people are at least as civilised as people on the mainland. But nor is Ulster imposed on and plundered by Britain—in fact Ulster receives massive subsidies from the British state. Ireland was not conquered by England 700 years ago, as Eire's propaganda holds, and far from wanting to hang on to Ulster, the British policy has been to pull out of it as soon as possible. Britain only remains there owing to the majority's demands and actions in Ulster. Thatcher is not the first to try to sell out.

Yet the Republic of Ireland, on the other hand, would clearly be both an endarkening and a plundering imperialist power in Ulster. In addition to high taxation at the expense of the poor, and the religious impositions, Eire's police and courts are notorious for rough justice.

A one-year ultimatum

People in the UK have been taken in by Catholic propaganda and so desire to be rid of Ulster. They would probably vote to kick it out in a referendum. Would this be bad? Not necessarily: a one-year ultimatum that Ulster was going to be cut from Mother Britain's apron strings would give the Ulster people time to marshal their defences. (The IRA was only allowed to grow by the natural defences of Ulster being banned in 1969 when the troops were called in to protect the Catholics.) A small border war, killing mainly volunteer soldiers, might then ensue between Ulster and the South. The Irish war would not last long. Ulster's borders would be redefined. The South would slowly come to terms with the fact that they are not going to be allowed to rule (by majoritarian democracy) over the North (where countless opinion polls show that less than half of even the Catholic minority currently support joining the Republic). The Republic would save face and be considerably consoled by Britain's absence from Ulster (and that they would probably gain more Catholic-inhabited land than they would lose). The majority of people on the mainland see Ireland as one nation and a thorn in Britain's side to be got rid of somehow; the Unionists want to remain connected to Britain and see an independent Ulster as a poor second best, but being controlled by Eire as absolutely out of the question: an independent Ulster is eventually inevitable. A one-year ultimatum would minimise bloodshed by avoiding both the type of sudden withdrawal that caused massacres in India and Pakistan, and a futile attempt to force Ulster into Eire's control.

Hanging now ...

Only gratuitous violence is barbaric. Mrs Thatcher is wrong to think that these Eire terrorists need merely to be "deprived of the oxygen of publicity". They do not aim at publicity; they aim at the conquest of Northern Ireland. Literally depriving them of oxygen would help in the short run. Ulster alone is far better able to take care of terrorism. Terrorism will be crushed in double quick time as soon as the Ulster people accept the need to defend themselves. Terrorism survives largely because politicians succumb to the still fashionable prejudice against capital punishment. But if you raise the price of terror then less will be bought. (The IRA's self-imposed deaths, by suicide in 1981, did dramatically end and it showed no sign of restarting.) Politicians on the front line, as in Ulster, will not risk so-called humane policies against bombers and gunmen.

... enlightenment later

But the remedy of capital punishment deals only with the symptoms of the violence. Most problems are those of ignorance, and enlightenment is the cure. This is the case with the Republic of Ireland. The long-term solution to terrorism in this case is for Eire to realise that its activities are futile and illegitimate—and so abandon them. (People never try to do what they fully realise to be futile, by definition.) The South has to see that it cannot take Ulster, for Ulster is too strong: the Ulster people are fighting for their survival on home ground whilst the Republic has few imperialists as fanatical as the IRA. The South also has to see that they have no right to Ulster, even by their own nationalist standards: the Protestants are not the remnants of an imposed Ascendancy, as Eire likes to think, but form a separate and older nation. (The Anglo-Irish Ascendancy was made up of the ruling classes of Britain in Ireland. It ruled southern Gaels and Northern Presbyterians alike. It was substantially withdrawn at the turn of the century, leaving a new nation in the south and a strong Irish, but Unionist, society in the north.)

A deregulated Ulster

Separate from the UK, Ulster could expand its economy to a position of completely unassailable affluence by declaring itself a tax haven; say with taxes at a maximum of 20%. Lower VAT in Ulster currently attracts many Southern Irish shoppers. It seems likely that lower taxes overall would attract businesses generally. Abolishing the rent acts would bring more property onto the market to cope with the new people coming to Ulster. All further steps towards deregulating the economy would encourage further investment, and they would probably end up with a goodly number of British immigrants if they tried this. They would attract even more Eire immigrants. Ulster could become as big a success as Hong Kong, or Singapore, or Iceland, if they would only do some of the things that Mrs Thatcher merely talks about. Having so few people is not a problem: Iceland with less than 250,000 people has the highest standard of living in Europe. (They also have a thriving libertarian movement.)

This vision might appear improbable to many. Northern Ireland seems as sold on the welfare-warfare state as is Britain. But the Reverend Ian Paisley, the next prime minister of Ulster, has made some favourable noises about liberalising the economy in the past. He might see this as the only way forward without British handouts. The people of Ulster might be forced to liberalise initially if they are to survive. They might then see the benefits of this liberalisation and want to keep it. This is happening with free trade zones in China and the Philippines.

State welfare-warfare 'insurance'

But isn't Ulster insured with Britain for protection purposes just like the Falklands? And shouldn't we treat welfare payments in Ulster just like high welfare payments in Liverpool? No: they are not insured for welfare nor for warfare purposes.

The idea of "national insurance contributions" through taxation is quite foolish. Taxation is coercively taken money none of which is invested. That money is squandered by the government. When you want health care and other state services the state taxes you (and other people) again to pay for it. This is not insurance. There is no reason why the people of Ulster couldn't insure themselves properly, and at less cost, for private health care, defence, and other services at present provided by the British state. The prices for these things would fall dramatically in a deregulated and temporarily poorer Ulster.

It would have been wrong for the British government suddenly to refuse to help the Falkland Islanders when they were invaded, because the government had, over the years, taught them to rely on the British state (though Thatcher was preparing to give the Falklands to Argentina in slow stages, when Galtieri got impatient). But it would be right and proper to slowly withdraw support now, so that they can gradually take up economic, private insurance (if they can afford it). It would be equally unwise suddenly to withdraw from Ulster without fair notice—a one-year ultimatum.

Liverpool is on a par with Ulster in terms of being an unwarranted parasite upon other people in the UK (though Ulster cost 1.4 billion pounds last year and Liverpool only a small fraction of this). It is irrelevant that people in these formerly prosperous areas once subsidised, through taxation, other British backwaters. That was a complete waste as well. The people of Ulster and of Liverpool should have no legitimate claim to the earnings of others. And they lose much more by state regulations that destroy competition, than they gain in handouts.

Nationalism is the problem

The long-term problem in Ireland has been competing nationalisms. The long-term solution to nationalism in Ireland, like everywhere else, is complete free-market anarchy: where each person's home is their castle and no one tries to impose his values on other groups; where people pay for competing private protection agencies to protect themselves and their personal property from force and fraud. This solution is a long way off. Much more free-market propaganda is necessary first (this article is not intended to put the general case for market anarchy). In the meantime, an Ulster nation of people generally providing for themselves—not imposing on or being imposed on by other nations—is a more liberal solution all round than would be rule from either Westminster or Dublin.

7) Ulster: Cut the Apron Strings

(A reply to David Ramsay Steele from *Free Life*, vol. 5, no. 3, 1987.[1])

The article on Ulster ('Ulster: Troops Out - Market In', *Free Life*, vol. 4, no. 3) might look confused, especially if taken with Berry and McDonagh's article on the Falklands as background. Part of the apparent confusion is because McDonagh's name appears mainly as a result of his contribution of the sections on historical outline ('The Two Irish Nations in Context', 'How Eire was Born', and 'The Irish Question'), although he did make critical contributions to the rest of the piece. The signing of the article is there to show authorship, not to guarantee sincerity. Neither author can honestly say that he fervently believes everything in the article. The authors' beliefs are irrelevant to the rightness of what is written. But we do happen to believe that the arguments put down are worth considering, or we should not have written them. Thus some of the charges Steele makes against McDonagh for signing inconsistent theses seem misconceived. But the remaining criticisms will be dealt with here.

Ambivalent to the orthodox

There is no basic ambivalence in the thesis of the essay. The argument is against Irish Nationalism and Ulster Unionism; and in favour of Ulster Nationalism. On an orthodox nationalistic outlook it must look odd to assert that Ulster is really culturally British but then state that it ought to be jettisoned from the UK. Why argue for Britishness if only to go on to argue for separation? Because even a non-nationalist can use nationalist arguments to reduce the Irish Nationalists claims to absurdity. The first thesis—as argued for mainly in McDonagh's sections—is intended to do just that. The Irish Nationalist case is self-undermining. Ulster is culturally British, and that prevents it from being identified as one nation with Eire (as we called the South). Some libertarians are content to let the matter stop there. But this hardly seems a very libertarian answer to the 'Irish Question'. Of course Ulster Nationalism is not a completely libertarian answer either, but it was argued that it would be more liberal than having Ulster live off external taxpayers whilst being forced to tolerate chronic terrorism.

Goodbye Falklands

Yes, with the Falklands a similar pull-out policy to that advocated for Ulster should eventually be possible and desirable. It is currently even less politically acceptable and desirable than trying this with Ulster, but by propaganda it might eventually become so. If we deny this then we seem to be committed to saying that taxpayers in Britain must be obliged to pay to defend anywhere British in perpetuity as long as the people there demand it.

It is not suggested that Falklands or Ulster should he given up just because there is a foreign claim on them. Nor is it suggested that they should end up in the hands of those who claim them. It would be good to see Britain push out all subsidised regions were that possible (goodbye Liverpool, goodbye Scotland ...) with a view to the eventual complete dismantling of the British nation-state. True, we (the Libertarian Alliance) are aiming to change society to libertarianism by converting the majority in the long run; but some self-perceived state beneficiaries are bound to be pushed out before they get around to seeing the virtue of leaving.

This is not suggested in the belief that foreign powers would simply take over, but in the belief that the subsidies are uneconomic and that efficient voluntary, free-market defence would replace state provision. The small size of the areas need be no obstacle to provision of defence. It is not suggested that only the indigenous populations with self-sufficient resources must be allowed to defend themselves. It is quite libertarian to opt for alliances of regional defence companies, global defence companies, or simply insurance with these. There is no reason that a given area need provide any of its own defence services. It might well prove economic for smaller areas like the Falklands to be insured with entirely external defence agencies. These might eventually include privatised armed forces in Britain (though these would not be 'British' in the statist sense).

Berry and McDonagh in their Falkland's piece (*Free Life*, vol. 3, no. 4) seem to be attempting to give the most practical liberal advice for the immediate future. They certainly demonstrate deep confusion and illiberal views on Rothbard's 'radical libertarian' position on the Falklands. Perhaps the alternatives here look just as bad as Rothbard's. But when asked what the specifically libertarian solutions to certain political problems are, one is often forced to paint a distant picture. Only by doing so will the picture ever stand a chance of coming nearer and eventually becoming realised. So "the solution that is in accordance with the wishes of the people concerned" (what of the taxpayers concerned who are against it?) certainly ought not to prevail forever if this means the unnecessary continuance of involuntarily subsidised inefficiency. Yet it has to be admitted that the above views might be being so far-sighted that they fail to convince by omitting sufficiently detailed directions on how to get there from here.

Overnight solution?

But what of Steele's proposed solution to the Irish question? This looks immediately impracticable. Steele suggests that the "British state ... could settle the whole question once and for all, almost overnight ... All that is needed is a convincing declaration that henceforth Ulster will stand in an administrative political relationship to Westminster somewhere between that of Wales and that of Humberside." This seems incredible. The IRA are ideologues motivated by a fervent moral-political vision. It is as though a conservative had suggested that the way to deal with libertarians once and for all is simply for the British State to issue a "convincing declaration" that it has no intention of ever dissolving itself.

Steele does not even concede that terrorism could be combated better in the short-run by a stronger deterrence in the form of the death sentence. The long-run campaign against the IRA has to be to convince them—or potential members—that they do not have right on their side, even in their own nationalistic terms. Another one of the ways of undermining their case is for Ulster to be clearly independent of Britain. Even the British State seems to see the ideological nature of the terrorism more clearly than does Steele.

A statist slogan

Appeal is made to "national self-determination". In itself this concept should not cut too much ice with a libertarian (Berry and McDonagh recognise many of the problems with this idea in their Falklands essay). For one thing, it is a slogan designed to legitimise nation-states. But if an external power really does make a society more liberal, then hurrah for that example of imperialism. In any case, whether national self-determination is achieved or not depends on where one draws the boundaries of the nation. The IRA can make out a good case that this is just the principle that they are fighting for: 'Ireland for the Irish.' And surely national self-determination does not allow a population "to attach itself to another nation-state" if that state does not want it; as is currently the case with Ulster and Britain.

Steele's California analogy seems an excellent one and it should help many people understand the situation better. There are two important factors missing in it though, which are chief culprits in causing the confusion: that there is a single island of Ireland (but not California), and that everyone on it describes themselves as Irish (but they do not all call themselves Mexican in California). Of course there is no more precise analogy around and this cannot be helped. So the irrelevance of these factors has to he argued separately: there are, for instance, three nations on the island adjacent to the island of Ireland, and that is not considered a problem; so one can be English-British, Welsh-British, Scottish-British and Irish-British.

Reasons to be sanguine

Steele lists the reasons given for advocating a one-year ultimatum of withdrawal from Ulster. But he misses the most important reason: the lack of British intervention would be crucial in undermining the ideological case of the IRA. Ireland would be for the Irish and the whole world would be able to see it. This would undermine the IRA's (and potential new recruit's) sense of righteous struggle. And to the extent that they still continued they would increasingly be seen by the rest of the world as themselves an 'imperialistic' force. External material and moral support for the IRA would dry up considerably.

In response to criticisms of the idea that the South would come to terms with their inability to subjugate an independent Ulster:

1. The main reason is the above mentioned undermining of the ideological position.
2. A considerable factor would also be that an armed and marshalled Ulster would be a much more vigorous and ready opponent than is Britain.
3. Steele mentions another reason only to dismiss it: the hope that Britain can help manipulate Ulster into a United Ireland. Steele is right to say that they ought to be able to see that this is not on the cards. Ulster will not allow it. He is right to say that many must be able to see this. But presumably IRA bombings are due to those members who cannot see this or they would not engage in them. It does not look on the face of it as though these acts of terrorism are working. Many IRA members must see the Anglo-Irish agreement as a concession in part brought about by the Brighton bombing—and they would be right. (Oddly, Steele himself calls this terrorism "sensible and rational" in his California analogy.) The UK-integration alternative that Steele suggests would strengthen their resolve and increase sympathy and assistance to them.

Many Catholics do not want integration with the South. They are not a threat now and need not be if an Ulster state is set up. Those who are currently a threat would be less troublesome given the harsher treatment that terrorists are bound to receive. If these populations looked as though they might be a problem, then one solution might well be to cede certain territory rather than kick out the occupants. This might be a considerable sweetener for the South. It would also, as stated in the original essay, help them to save face. But even if we suppose that Catholic populations were to be moved, it is not clear why this would make the small border war scenario "over-sanguine". If the Catholics really are a threat then moving them would bring a more stable peace that much sooner (the process of forcibly moving them would be highly undesirable from a libertarian viewpoint, but many might accept compensation if it were to be offered).

In response to criticism of the idea that an Ulster government can better deal with terrorism. Ulster alone would be better at fighting the IRA not by moving whole Catholic populations, but because they would rigorously seek out and execute terrorists. Despite the ideological fervour of the IRA this is bound to make the game a lot less attractive (especially to those not yet committed who would otherwise become the next generation of terrorists).

In response to the criticism that independence need not lead to deregulation:

> 1. Ulster is not a cultural island. It shares most aspects of culture with the mainland. One of these is the new movement to liberalism (though this is more or less a world-wide phenomenon). So there is a good reason for thinking that Ulster would not introduce extreme state-intervention.
> 2. There has been talk of liberalisation if they do split off from Britain. Paisley, in particular, has made such remarks.
> 3. They will be forced to liberalise to some extent in any case for they do not have the wealth to continue the level of state spending that they currently suffer.
> 4. Once they see the benefits—thanks to these new, liberal spectacles—they might well decide to have more of the same.

In response to the idea that it would be easier to abolish subsidies than eject Ulster:

One answer to the problem of subsidies to Ulster is to abolish all state subsidies. But this looks much less likely than merely abolishing Ulster's subsidies because Ulster has become independent. The abolition of all state subsidies would be tantamount to the complete abolition of the state. State subsidies are a major factor in giving the modem state moral legitimacy. A one-year ultimatum to Ulster is a far greater possibility than similar ultimata to "Liverpool, Glasgow, Lambeth, Cornwall, and so forth." But given that libertarian anarchy requires the eventual dismantling of the nation-state, then such ultimata ought not to be ruled out in principle as potential good routes in some cases.

Ulster as a whole is a drain on the resources of the mainland according to all reports at the time of the Anglo-Irish agreement. An initial figure of 4 billion pounds turned out to be 1.4 billion net. Given the high levels of unemployment, council housing, state employment, policing, and army requirements—in addition to all the usual state consumption—a net subsidy hardly seems remarkable.

Death to the Union

Steele gives two reasons that a policy of integration with the UK is superior to expulsion. First he claims that the bulk of Ulster citizens want it and almost none of them wants independence. But this is to neglect what is wanted by the majority of people they wish to impose it on. Then he claims that integration would improve community relations whereas an Ulster nation would make every Catholic suspect. This is to fail to see that far from being stamped out and undermined (as would be the case with separation) Irish nationalism would be fuelled for many years to come.

The expulsion of Ulster is described as "something horrible". But the alternative that Steele prescribes looks worse. We know what the horrors of terrorism are like, and we can expect a lot more of them if there are any moves towards full Ulster integration with the UK. Mainland bombings decreased after the Anglo-Irish agreement; they can be expected to increase dramatically at any sign of a reverse. But if Britain were out of the problem then there would be no incentive to attack the mainland and decreased incentives to attack Ulster itself

The abolition of Stormont and increased Ulster representation in Westminster has to be weighed against the Anglo-Irish agreement and any further plans that the British politicians have in mind if we wish to see whether Ulster is more firmly within the UK than ever. The people of Ulster probably doubt an increase in the security of the Union.

A referendum about 'the Irish'

A referendum is bound to change some people's minds about Ulster, but the situation is probably too complicated for a relatively uninterested majority to get to grips with it. The 'Irish Question' would not be perceived to be about the British. The easy and popular ideas are that 'Ireland should be for the Irish', and that 'the Irish are a thorn in our side': 'costing us money, bombing us, killing our boys'. These ideas would take a lot to be refuted. There is little sympathy for the Unionist case outside fringe Conservative groups. Paisley himself is something of a hate figure among media people and they seem typical in this. The final attitude is likely to be that it is far easier to 'give the elbow to the lot of them'.

But even if the majority of Brits wanted to keep Ulster in the UK what right would they have to impose this cost even on a minority who do not want to support them? Such democratic arguments ought not to carry much weight with a libertarian. The majority of Brits want the NHS, but that does not make it right that the minority who do not want it are forced to contribute.

This combination of nationalistic and democratic arguments sounds very odd in the mouths of libertarians. Perhaps they would make a better case if they could come up with more libertarian arguments (but the idea of increased British-state involvement with a subsidised, under-protected Ulster has an anti-liberal ring to it). Part of the problem seems to be an ideological myopia: that the best way forward is to offer immediate political policies rather than say where you really want to get to. The Adam Smith Institute is founded on this error—although it is not thereby utterly useless—but the LA usually takes a wiser, long-sighted and frank approach. Perhaps what has really happened is that some LA members have swallowed whole the British and Irish Communist Organisation's—admittedly superior—analysis. They ought to allow a little libertarian digestion to take place.

Note

[1] For David Ramsay Steele's article see the same issue of *Free Life*, vol. 5, No. 3, Libertarian Alliance online.

8) AIDS: Not "Everyone's Problem"

(From *Free Life*, vol. 5, no. 1, 1987.)

Why is the government spreading AIDS and lying about its being "everyone's problem"? AIDS is certainly not "everyone's problem", and so far as it looks it never will be. AIDS is very hard to catch by vaginal, heterosexual intercourse. Sexual infection with AIDS normally requires that the body fluids of a carrier enter some abrasion or cut in the partner. This very rarely occurs with vaginal intercourse (the vagina and penis being sturdier than the rectum and anus). Infected blood transfusions on the NHS, and heroin users sharing hypodermic needles because the state bans their sale, have been two other major routes for the virus (though all blood donations are now tested). There is also some risk from oral sex. The statistics, largely gleaned from *The Independent* (*12/1/87*) and *Newsweek* (*19/1/87*), bear this out. Both are good examples of the media toeing the government line and thereby ignoring or misinterpreting their own evidence.

Who gets AIDS?

The AIDS virus is rife in Africa. In Uganda, as many as one in ten are infected, according to *The Independent*. Men and women have it about in equal numbers. But Africa has differences that make it highly unlikely that Europe could reach the same state. The Africans have mostly spread the disease by open sores on their genitalia due to untreated venereal disease. These diseases are between 10 and 100 times more common in Africa. They have other diseases that weaken their immune systems. Insanitary medical treatment, especially dirty needles, also seems to be the cause of infection. That buggery is not the main cause of infection in Africa now seems likely, for there is relatively little anal syphilis and gonorrhoea compared with the genital cases (though buggery of both sexes is quite popular among Africans according to a Kenyan I once knew).

In the US and France the number of heterosexual victims is creeping up (25% in France says *Newsweek*) but the bulk of these seem to be either immigrants (French-speaking Africans in the French case) who have come for superior medical treatment, or hypodermic-needle-users (these state-caused cases actually outnumber the anal-sex cases in Italy and Scotland). Of the 30,000-odd US deaths, 500 (one sixtieth) were native Americans who got it via heterosexual intercourse, and fewer than a hundred were men. Heterosexual intercourse, logically, ought to include the highly risky anal intercourse with a woman, but they omit to explain this crucial point. This could be AIDS spreading to heterosexuals slowly via women who have had promiscuous bisexual partners. But this trend would probably level off due mainly to the relative safety of vaginal, heterosexual intercourse. The gay capital, San Francisco, will probably remain the AIDS capital that it has now also become.

Figures collected by the New York City health department, cited in *The Spectator,* 14/2/87, flatly contradict that journal's moralistic, self-righteous doom mongering:

> Whereas the number of new cases doubled in 1983, it only went up 20% in 1986, meaning that the curve is getting flatter, not steeper. Only 3% of the current patients, broadly classified as heterosexuals, do not belong to the high-risk groups. The health department says it believes most of this 3% fraction actually belong to high-risk groups but deny it. Of the remaining handful, two thirds are black and Hispanic heterosexuals who live in ghetto areas where intravenous drug use is rife.

In the UK, there are only four people known to have the AIDS virus (but not the disease) as a result of heterosexual (vaginal?) sex, and two of these are female prostitutes. Generally, AIDS is very rare even among prostitutes, and it would be rarer still except that some do allow anal sex without a condom. More significantly perhaps, prostitutes are also often intravenous heroin users driven to share scarce needles. Only about 50 heterosexuals have come up positive in the AIDS virus test in the UK. These are mostly partners of high-risk victims: haemophiliacs, drug users and bisexuals. But there are 3,877 gays that are positive, though promiscuous gays constitute a very small percentage of the population. Of the 610 people in Britain who have the actual disease, at least 538 of them are admitted homosexuals or bisexuals.

It looks even safer for heterosexual men than for heterosexual women. A heterosexual man will not be buggered while the woman might be, and the vagina might be a good environment in which the disease can get a hold: for one thing, open blood vessels can occur during menstruation. Unless one has an open sore on one's penis, it is very hard to catch AIDS as the active partner when having intercourse with the infectious carrier. In a study in the States of persistent intercourse without condoms with an AIDS-carrying spouse, 16% of wives have eventually caught it from their infected husbands, and a mere 5% of husbands have caught it from their infected wives. Nobody caught it when condoms were worn.

So, in the UK you can still get AIDS from sharing the hypodermic needles that are state-restricted, but usually one has to bend over forwards in order to catch the disease. One also needs to bend over regularly, indiscriminately, and without one's partners wearing condoms. Not so much a "gay plague", then, as a "promiscuous, passive, anal-intercourse plague".

Why the big lie?

Why is this lie that "AIDS is everyone's problem" being spread at great public expense? The "moral" right are on the offensive. AIDS is the punishment for all the wicked activities they despise: not just homosexuality, but promiscuity as such, and drug taking. The "moral" left are on the defensive. They want to defend homosexuals from persecution, having latched onto them as one of their pet minorities. Many gays may be happy to accept this defence. But, this ploy looks designed to backfire: people can see that gays have the disease and that heterosexuals, by-and-large, do not; it might lead them to shun the "dangerous" homosexuals who spread this "universal" plague.

Then there are the doom mongers who revel in the fact that they have discovered yet another way in which the world is certain to end along with a nuclear winter, or is it a scorching summer? Or is it aerosol cans? Or is it too few trees? Or is it too many people? ... Or are these merely doom mongers? The main problem is the politicians who so desperately want to be seen to be useful. They would be blamed by the "moral" alliance, doom mongers and the opposition for whatever follows unless they "do something" about this "crisis".

Why don't the government advertisements give us the less than volcanic statistics? Because then we would all clearly see it is more dangerous in this part of the world to cross the road than to engage in promiscuous-condomless-vaginal intercourse. Some such comparison is always useful to put such problems into perspective. Young people are quite rightly ignoring this AIDS scare, as they so sensibly ignored the nonsense about heroin being so dangerous. They have first-hand experience that no promiscuous heterosexuals are catching the disease.

Unfortunately, when the government gets to hear about this, they are simply going to use it as an excuse to spend more of other people's money on their big lie. People can come to believe big lies if they shun the evidence— and even if they don't, apparently: *The Independent* had plenty of evidence but it sandwiched the truth between the ridiculous title "Heterosexuals face slow march of AIDS", and the conclusion that 'it is now everybody's problem'. Perhaps they believe that they will lose popularity if they consistently contradict the big lie. *Newsweek* certainly seems to have this attitude; it took four reporters to say absolutely nothing about body fluids needing to enter the blood and why buggery is, therefore, particularly dangerous. Instead they clearly implied that any promiscuity spreads AIDS. Yet in the next article (on possible treatment) they dismissively mention James Curran, the Director of the AIDS programme at the Centre for Disease Control (in Atlanta), for his view that gays and intravenous drug users are the real problem.

On the evidence so far it seems that AIDS is so easily avoided that it will probably level off in Europe and the States even if no cure is forthcoming (gays were changing their habits long before the misleading government advertisements). But there will probably still be enough of it about to ensure that the drug companies will feverishly seek a cure (without taxpayers' subsidies). The same profit motive in the media will ensure that we are kept up to date on the topic, globally and locally. If a real and local risk to heterosexuals should arise then they would be the first to tell us. In the meantime, it can do no good for the government to cry wolf, ration hypodermic needles and throw our money around (only 20 million so far, but with another 15 million here and 25 million there pretty soon we are talking about real money). It will buy politicians some votes but it will do us no good. These nasty little vote grubbers cannot accept the, so often appropriate, advice: don't just do something—sit there!

9) The Market for Justice

(From *Free Life*, vol. 5, no. 2, 1987.)

Should all murderers be hanged? Should all car firms produce red cars? These are both matters on which laymen like you, me, the newspapers, politicians and high-court judges are quite incompetent to decide for everyone else. In the free market the punishment for criminals would depend on what satisfies the consumers. Thus in the UK, private courts would he likely to compete to supply punishments geared to efficient deterrence and restitution, as these seem fair and safe to most of us. The precise levels and methods of punishment that made for the best deterrence would be researched by professionals and continuously tested by market competition.

With hanging (or gladiatorial combat on pay-TV) the level of risk to the convicted but innocent would be pointed out. The self-interested consumers might well prefer to take the tiny risk of being killed by a miscarriage of justice, rather than the much larger risk of being murdered because of insufficient deterrence. But some might not prefer this. They might consider it always immoral to kill. And in the market one could always take out a policy that allowed one's own murderer to have a lesser punishment than death.

A vengeful few might desire extreme retribution for relatively minor crimes. They would accept the high price in terms of personal risks from both the criminals (who reason that they might as well he hanged for a sheep as a lamb) and their own protection company (which might mistakenly convict them). But to enforce these sentences they would probably have to congregate in areas where they owned all the property.

Contractual justice

Yet how is any punishment justified from within the market-libertarian viewpoint? Not because it deters and provides restitution—though these do seem likely to be seen as the safest and most moral, and so the most popular criteria of choice—but because the criminal opts in with a quasi-contract. The diner in the restaurant tacitly contracts to pay the bill later though there is no explicit agreement; the burglar quasi-contracts to be liable to be punished for his burglary. He chooses to consume the crime, and should pay the local going price.

We should replace the state's arbitrary monopoly of justice. The market would give us a system of justice based on informed, individual choices where we (innocent and criminal) bear our own costs. What could be more moral and efficient?

10) Market Libertarianism Entails Quasi-Contracts: a Reply to Jonathan LeCocq[1]

(From *Free Life*, vol. 6, no. 1, 1988.)

At the end of *"Justice for Sale"* (*Free Life*, vol. 5, no. 2) I asked how any punishment is justified from within the market-libertarian viewpoint. This is different from asking for an underpinning of the viewpoint (which I also gave some ideas on). I accept Jon LeCocq's idea (*Free Life*, vol. 5, no. 3) that a more basic argument than my own for punishing criminals is that a society without such punishment would be less free generally. But we might push the argument back further still and argue that we want more such overall freedom because it makes for more welfare (I might then defend this welfarist position as a fundamental moral assumption). It is fair comment to point out that a defence of a position is less fundamental than it might be. But it is not necessarily a fault to ignore more basic principles. Always to use them would soon become tedious and might fail to give people the flavour of the new mode of thought that one wants to convey.

In a libertarian society legal controversy would not focus on utilitarian considerations. The welfare superiority would have to be a background assumption for the most part. Neither would law focus on what maximises overall freedom, for that would also make for a philosophical level of discussion that would be out of place in ordinary dealings. The quasi-contractual view of crime and punishment was being offered as an argument for those people who already take the value of liberty for granted but who see all punishment as rather like the initiation of aggression. I argued that it is more like the enforcement of a contract, so libertarians do not need to be so uneasy about punishment. When asked if we can give a demonstration that punishment leads to a freer society overall we can first reply that it is *part* of a free society (in the libertarian sense) that contracts are enforced, and enforcing such quasi-contracts is also a part.

On the face of things, then, the libertarian view ought conceptually to comprise this attitude to punishment rather than to have it as a mere contingent method of realising contractarian liberty. A society without punishment according to the levels that people pay to see enforced would be less free. But it would be less free not merely because the absence of the *contingent* "deterrent and restrictive effects of punishment". It would be less free because to deny people the right to 'price' crimes as they choose to would necessarily violate the properly-contractual conception of freedom. To put a limit on permissible punishment is analogous to putting limits on the price of any product in the market. We can defend quasi-contractual punishment with the same sorts of arguments that we use to attack price controls. But my real point is logical rather than contingent. So if it is correct then it is even more 'safe' than the approach Mr LeCocq suggests.

I do not suggest that with quasi-contractual punishment "this coercion is in one sense no coercion". Coercion is force and threat of force, and punishment usually involves that. But such punishment is not the violation of libertarian property rights; it is the enforcement of them. It is reactive rather than proactive coercion.

We are told that a "contract requires consent and there are no partners." But it is obvious that there are partners to this quasi-contract: the criminal and the person who 'charges the price' for the crime against him. A diner's intention and willingness to pay has nothing to do with whether he has a contract or not. Even if he always intended to run from the restaurant he would still have a (tacit) contract. I suggest that the same applies to criminals.

I do not hold that quasi-contracts occur by one simply putting oneself into a situation where something is liable to happen. Going for a walk late at night does not produce a quasi-contract to be mugged, because the mugger does not have any moral right to what he takes. The correctness of libertarian property rights is presupposed. If it were not then there might be a good analogy between the mugger and the muggee.

A criminal who chooses to commit crimes in a society with Draconian punishments would not be able to find an agency to protect him—or it would not be such a society. Similarly, individuals who chose to live in gentler societies would not find an agency to enforce amputation of a hand for theft. I do not see that individuals would be able to dictate just any price they like, any more than they could insist that someone buy a car from them at ten times the going rate. There would be a quasi-market price for punishments, and if they didn't like it they would have to go elsewhere.

In some sense the individual's property rights are being overridden by the majority here, but without this people could not set up alternative societies if they wished to—and to live in such a society in the first place is to quasi-contract into the rules that they enforce. I did not state that "no individual is entitled to decide for any other" on the question of punishment; I stated that we are individually "quite incompetent to decide for everyone else". I admit that there is a majoritarian element to the market, but it is not as arbitrary as democracy (or any other system of rule), and people can more easily set up separate communities in competition.

Note

[1] For Jonathan LeCocq's article see *Free Life*, vol. 5, no. 3, Libertarian Alliance online.

11) Glib Glossary: a Random and Ironic Guide to Social Thought

(From *Free Life*, vol. 5, no. 3, 1987.)

The Market (I): A terrifying system of anarchistic order whereby people interact voluntarily to achieve ends by mutual gain.

The State (I): A reassuring system of planned chaos whereby people initiate coercion to achieve ends by mutual predation.

The Market (2): An iniquitous system of social organisation whereby the weak commodities are allowed to perish simply to raise the living standards of human beings.

The State (2): A benevolent organisation that extorts 'protection' money under threat of seizure of property or kidnapping and incarceration.

Socialist: A vicarious philanthropist who wishes to be charitable with other people's money.

Tory: A dogmatic, ideological, paternalist who thinks he is a rational, pragmatic, paternalist.

Communist: A radical Tory.

Patriot: Someone who thinks the state created the indigenous flora and fauna, and that these benefit from occasional feeding with the natives' blood.

(Classical) Liberal/Libertarian: Believer in the right of each to be the slave of none.

Democrat: Believer in the duty of each to be the slave of all.

(Modern) 'Liberal': See Democrat.

Dogmatism: The refusal to entertain criticism.

'Dogmatist': The dogmatist's label for people with opinions at odds with his own.

Dogmatic Ideologue: One who holds that ideologically correct means justify the ends, though the heavens fall.

Pragmatic Ideologue: One who holds that desirable ends justify certain ideological means— what else could?

Selfishness: The immoral folly of living unduly for oneself.

Selflessness: The immoral folly of living unduly for others.

Self-interest: The natural virtue of caring for oneself.

Altruism: The natural virtue of caring for others.

Discrimination: Observing differences, making a distinction, observing distinctions carefully, acute discernment.

Reverse/positive discrimination: Discriminating against white men.

Feminism: Very confusingly, this is either an anti-feminine movement (denigrating uncoerced female behaviour), or an anti-masculine movement (denigrating uncoercive male behaviour). This apparent contradiction is reconciled by realising that the motive for 'feminism' is usually a Procrustean dislike of sexual differences.

Moralise: The expression of sentiments concerning some type of behaviour regardless of anyone's immediate personal interests. A natural human disposition, but without any particular content.

'Moralise': To bore an immoral person by moralising.

Moral/Immoral: That which is (to be) approved/disapproved of as a type of behaviour regardless of immediate personal interests.

'Objectively Moral/Immoral': My morals/your morals.

'Justice': The enforcement of some system of laws that is objectively moral because I say it is.

'Social justice': Apparently a contraction of 'socialist justice'; the enforcement of a social system of laws that only the extremely evil, cretinously ignorant, or certifiably insane would oppose.

Microeconomics: A new name for economics since Keynes.

Macroeconomics: The development of spurious arguments for state meddling in the economy.

'Privatise': The radical policy of turning an inefficient state-regulated monopoly into an inefficient state-regulated monopoly. (*See* British Telecom)

Deregulate: The wicked anarchistic policy of allowing free competition to lower prices and improve services.

Sociology: The study of society.

'Sociology': The study of society using defunct economic theories, or at least avoiding economic analysis. This partly explains the complete lack of useful knowledge generated by state-funded sociologists. The other part of the explanation is that society is studied by everyone as a matter of course, so it is difficult to come by extraordinary insights.

Hooliganism: The spectator sport of 'sociologists'. If your country is without this diverting pastime, here is a simple recipe for its production: deny male youths the time-consuming responsibility and satisfaction of paid employment until they are sixteen; then pay them not to work, all the while ensuring that state police detection is feeble and state legal penalties against violent destruction are derisory.

Political Science/Politics/Government: The study of the role of the state.

'Political Science/Politics/Government': The attempt to justify a role for the state by ignoring economics in favour of mystical worship of the nation, community, civil society, ...

'Doctor': A physician rather than a metaphysician; a medic; a body mechanic; a leech. After six years apprenticeship their services are so valuable that the public commonly needs to be tax-bled to support them (for people are supposed to be too stupid to insure themselves or buy medical care); only their intensive training enables them to declare a runny nose a cold, and spots acne. Cheaper, quicker-trained nurses or pharmacists have to be denied any diagnostic role 'in the public interest' if there is the slightest chance whatsoever that they might make a mistake (doctors never make mistakes), no matter what the cost in terms of the death, suffering, and expense of restricting this care to a profession.

Profession: A lucrative state-backed racket whereby the public is denied competition among some group of suppliers and often forced to pay their wages.

Drug abuser: Someone who makes bigoted gibes about drugs other than the ones he enjoys.

'Madman': Someone a dogmatist does not understand, does not want to understand, and does not want anyone else to understand.

12) The Market for Free Speech (or 'Free Speech: is Rushdie for it?')

(From *Free Life*, vol. 6, no. 2, 1989.)

Salman Rushdie does not believe in 'free speech'. Neither did most of the literati asked for their opinions on his circumstances in *The New Statesman and Society* (31 March, 1989). What they did generally support is the right of authors to have what they write published—well, they would, wouldn't they? They did not mention that—as typical western statists—they are in favour of all manner of other types of state regulation of communication. To be fair, such double standards are partly due to a common confusion about the nature of 'free speech' and ignorance of how private property is relevant.

Free communication

It is surely in the spirit of the expression 'free speech' that it includes freedom of all communication; that is Morse code, pictures, and so forth. In this sense 'pornography' (depiction of sexual practices, whether verbally or visually, felt to be indecent by the speaker) is as much an exercise of 'free speech' as 'blasphemy' (disparaging the religion of the speaker). For the state to restrict either of these is against the more general and useful notion of 'free communication'.

'Free speech' has two important senses that are often confused. They are confused because they are closely related. One sense is personal while the other is political. The personal sense means 'anti-dogmatism'. When people claim to practise free speech they mean they are willing to give a hearing to their opponents. The political sense means 'no state interference with voluntary communication'. In no country in the world does a state tolerate full voluntary communication. In the UK, TV and radio are almost as restricted as in the USSR; very few channels are allowed and these are heavily regulated.

Clearly, one can believe in complete free speech in the political sense while choosing to avoid debate in one's own life. The libertarian view has to be that it is wrong for the state, or anyone, to interfere with voluntary communication, but that people should be at liberty (within free-market property rights) to send or shun any communication. This not only means that the state *ought not to prevent* any voluntary communications, but that *neither ought it to impose* communications (on television stations, radios, newspapers, notice boards; at work, school, or in the street, whether by the IBA, Party Political Broadcasts, 'public information' campaigns. or core curricula).

Why private solutions?

It is sometimes held that free speech has to be limited for the good of all. The classic examples are shouting "Fire!" in a crowded (non-burning) theatre, and inciting a crowd to violence. But in the context of free-market property rights, proscribing these need not mean making exceptions to freedom of communication. In the case of the theatre it is clear that the owners can demand certain standards of behaviour as part of the conditions of admittance; such disturbances can thus be contractually proscribed. In the case of private streets the situation is exactly the same. Street owners are going to avoid trouble by banning violence, threatening behaviour, or incitement to violence.

This approach would preclude such things as Nazi groups holding provocative rallies in predominantly Jewish areas (as happened in Skokie, USA, a few years ago) and black groups doing the same to annoy racist whites (as has also happened in the US). Both groups were allowed such provocation on the basis of freedom of speech and assembly, precisely thanks to the confusion over the two senses of 'free speech' and the lack of private property rights in streets. In a market society where the locals owned or were the major customers of streets, such provocation would be highly unlikely; businesses do not want to permanently alienate the majority of their best customers. Private ownership of all streets and open spaces lets the owners decide what shall be allowed and what forbidden— at the benefit and cost of the owners and contracting users.

This solution does not prevent people expressing their views elsewhere (in a journal, rented hall, or even hired—possibly distant— street or park). It preserves the desirable option of communicating to those who choose to receive the communication; it simply ensures that people do not enjoy expressing themselves at the inconvenience and expense of others.

It is unfortunate that some people are offended merely by what other people choose to communicate to each other within the limits of their own property. If person A is offended by what persons B and C are watching, reading or saying on their own property, then person A is worse off. But such distant offence is as nothing compared to the tangible destruction of welfare and wealth caused by person A's violently interfering with the voluntary behaviour of B and C. The state-regulators must learn to quell their own aggressive intolerance—if only to avoid engendering similar feelings against themselves. And even the relatively tolerant must learn that the only practical alternative to authoritarian censorship and propaganda is respect for private property.

13) The Right to Private Discrimination

(From *Free Life*, vol. 6, no. 3, 1990.)

Are people that are discriminated against thereby oppressed?

No: they are merely not benefited. You do not interfere with people by declining to offer them opportunities—whether these be opportunities to work for you or sleep with you. If you are not proactively interfering with people you cannot be oppressing them. But if you are legally obliged to offer others any such opportunities then *you* are being oppressed. To the extent that you cannot discriminate in the use of your property it ceases to be fully yours. Persecuting people because they belong to certain groups is certainly oppressive (to put it mildly), but the oppression lies in the positive interference and not in the discrimination as such.

Are people that discriminate against certain groups merely prejudiced?

No: prejudice means judging before examination; people that discriminate invariably have knowledge of their tastes and discriminate on the basis of these. If you prefer beer to cider, or chess to tennis, this is not mere prejudice. Similarly, we all discriminate among people for a variety of purposes based on our tastes. We can be mistaken about those we reject, but it is foolish for them to think we are likely to see our error by being forced to associate with them. The best chance of winning the acceptance of those one wishes to associate with is to avoid imposing on them.

Is discrimination by business, restaurants, etc., different because they serve the public?

No: these are private concerns and should not be for anyone's use without the permission of the private owner. Who comes into your business, your home, or your bed is entirely 'your business'. Only the activities of the state and any businesses it controls are 'public', in the sense that it is not a private matter when the state decides to discriminate against or in favour of certain groups: people are either oppressed or privileged to the extent that the state treats them unequally.

Do employers that discriminate on the basis of sex, race, religion, etc., use criteria irrelevant to the job?

No: jobs do not have objective requirements beyond what the employer wants. A business is a means to whatever ends its owner chooses. Employers have no more reason to be solely profit-maximisers than consumers have to buy only the cheapest goods. An employer can quite rationally choose to employ certain groups as his primary business purpose. Only the employer can decide what his purposes in his business are and what sort of people he wishes to employ. If a private employer prefers devout Muslims, or homosexual men, or one-legged Eskimos, then these qualifications are thereby relevant to the job. Naturally, employers do not usually discriminate without strong reason when profits are at stake. So there is no reason to think that any groups will find themselves without any work just because, some will not employ them.

Businessmen are an oppressed minority in various ways including being oppressed by being legally obliged to employ certain groups. The people that employers would have preferred to employ are also oppressed by being denied the jobs that they would otherwise have had. And to legally oblige an employer to accept groups that require special facilities or concessions at the same rates of pay as other workers is to give these groups a positive privilege: they do not pay their way; everyone else is forced to subsidise them.

Is there any sound defence of anti-discrimination legislation?

No: people should not be forcibly segregated, as they are under apartheid—but neither should they be forced to integrate. This is an example of swinging from one evil to a contrary evil. To the extent that it exists, compulsory association is at least as destructive of liberty and welfare as is compulsory segregation. Private discrimination is a civil liberty that does no harm and which we all want for ourselves; to deny it to others is completely illiberal. All anti-discrimination legislation should be repealed.

14) Free Trade in Human Body Parts

(From *Free Life*, vol. 6, no. 3, 1990.)

Banning the free trade in human body parts is short-sighted, disgusting, selfish, and misanthropically evil in effect.

Many people are suffering and some people are dying due to lack of human body-parts for transplants. Free trade is a completely voluntary solution that would bring an abundance of body-parts making suffering and death due to the lack of them virtually unknown. It would also release for other purposes the money spent on such expensive items as renal-dialysis machines. This must all seem a good thing to anyone who is not either confused or a complete misanthrope.

Not all transplant material need come from living donors; many people would contract to allow transplants after their deaths. A little financial incentive would quickly solve the problem of the current shortage of card-carrying donors. But where live-donors are preferable, the competition of a legalised open market would soon improve the standards for donors and recipients. Respectable agencies would invite independent tests of their health standards and honesty. It could even be economic (due to the new abundant supply) to guarantee a free replacement to, say, a kidney donor in the unlikely event of trouble with his remaining kidney.

It is certainly an unnecessary evil for the state to bully people into carrying donor cards or to impose cannibalisation after death, as some suggest. If people don't like the idea of being donors then there is no good reason to impose it on them given the infinitely superior voluntary alternative. And would you really feel safe in a hospital where doctors might be tempted to (at least) not try too hard to save you if your parts could, without your consent, save several others?

Obviously, a poorer person is more likely to sell his body-parts. He wants what others have and sees this as the best route to attaining that end. Those who oppose his actions are often much wealthier people motivated more by their own aesthetic distaste than by real moral sentiment or sympathy for the poor man who is trying to improve his lot. They don't offer to improve his life (as do those buying his body-parts) they simply want to stop this 'disgusting' practice. It is this selfish attitude of the wealthier that disgusts me.

But that is not the worst of it. Those who would ban the sale of your body-parts are thereby to some extent asserting their right to impose partial control over your body. They don't buy your body parts from you honestly; they simply stake a claim in deciding what you can do with them. This is replacing voluntary sale with partial slavery. And that is intolerable. Yet even that is not the real horror of it. The most important and tragic fact is that some people are being prevented from buying transplants where the foreseeable consequence is their death. If this is not murder then it is at least manslaughter.

Like all civilized people I am completely opposed to using violence—against the innocent. But what must we say of a person effectively sentenced to death in this way if, one dark night, he corners a politician who has voted to criminalize this voluntary trade and relieves him of the appropriate vital organ to save himself? Surely this can be no more than killing in self-defence.

15) No Representation Without Taxation!

(Libertarian Alliance online, 1995.)

The other day I saw some old film footage of Suffragettes marching with a banner that read, "Taxation Without Representation Is Tyranny". I seem to remember that some American colonials also once expressed similar views (whatever happened to them?). Most people would now regard that point as a fair one. I am no great fan of democracy, preferring liberty, but even I can agree that people who are taxed but not allowed to vote are likely to be more than averagely oppressed by those who can vote.

This then prompted me to consider the converse proposition: Representation Without Taxation Is Tyranny. It would, of course, be a fallacy to think that this is entailed by the first proposition. But surely it is just as reasonable. In the mid-nineteenth century most people accepted it as a fair limit on the franchise. Why should people who are not taxpayers be allowed to vote money away from those who are? If we must have state services, it should at least be for those who pay for them to vote for which services they want and how much they wish to pay. To allow those providing, or living off, the services to vote is like allowing a shopkeeper to vote on what you must buy from him, or a beggar to vote on what you must give him. Naturally, I hear you say, but doesn't everyone pay tax, at least on goods and services? And so is the proposition not true but irrelevant? No, they do not and it is not. Not by a very long chalk.

People in the pay of the state are not genuine taxpayers

Consider state distribution of tax-money. We can see that this must create two social categories: those who are net taxpayers and those who are net tax recipients. Only the net taxpayers can be said to provide the state with tax-funds. The net tax recipients are paid out of taxation, plus any payments in newly created state-currency (which effectively taxes those who hold money). So to the extent that people are in the pay of the state they cannot be genuine taxpayers. A proof of this is that if their jobs were abolished the state would have more money to spend elsewhere, unlike those jobs in the genuinely taxpaying sector.

To take a clear case, when a direct state-employee, such as a civil servant, receives his salary cheque, there will be an apparent deduction for the amount of tax that he pays. As a matter of fact this is a mere book-keeping exercise designed to keep up the pretence that he is a taxpayer along with everyone else. Abandoning this pretence of taxpaying and simply paying him less in the first place would save taxpayers' money in administration and make the political reality clearer to all.

An absolute injustice

Now, I am not arguing (here at least) that the people who live off taxation are social parasites. For the sake of argument, I am prepared to grant the (absurd) assumption of so many superior state services that the state ought to employ half the population. My point is that it should be clear who is paying what to whom and that those who are being paid cannot be allowed to decide what is to be paid for—which is what allowing them the vote does. This is an absolute injustice, a tyranny that destroys the wealth and liberty of the real taxpayers.

Class theory: true and false

Wouldn't allowing only taxpayers to vote be socially divisive? The social divide is there already. This is merely a demand that it be unmasked and that those who do not pay taxes be stripped of their privilege to vote themselves more 'resources' (as tax-recipients like to euphemise tax-money). Charles Comte, Charles Dunoyer, and Augustin Thierry were foremost among those who exposed this divide as the classical liberal theory of class. Yet Karl Marx took classical economics' supposed clash between labour and capital for his own notorious class theory. However, while there is sense to the idea that taxpayers and tax-recipients are at odds with each other (for every gain to the tax-recipient is a greater loss to the taxpayer in a destructive clash of interests), there is no truth in the idea that workers are at odds with capitalists (for there are gains to both sides, and to the consumer too, in the process of production). But if only the genuine taxpayers are voting for services that they want, then any conflict between the two tax-classes is minimised: taxpayers cannot be milked by tax-recipients (though there is still democracy's inevitable tyranny of the majority within the group of voting taxpayers).

Who doesn't and does pay taxes?

So who does not pay taxes and so ought not to have an electoral vote? Judges, state-school teachers, all in local government, state policemen, all in the armed forces, all in prison, all in the NHS, all in the civil service, all employees of the BBC, all the unemployed, all in academia (except, perhaps, in the private University of Buckingham), some farmers, some solicitors, maybe some barristers, any employed in businesses that receive tax-subsidies in excess of their tax-payments, and MPs with insufficient taxed market-incomes to cover their salaries. I cannot list them all, but you see the size of the problem. You can also see that there is no class conflict in any quasi-Marxian sense here.

Who, then, does pay taxes? Well, anyone who is left. If you are in any doubt as to which category that you are in then the simple test is to ask yourself whether, in your current position, you would have more purchasing power or less purchasing power if taxation were completely abolished.

The benefit of the doubt

There are some who are on the periphery of net tax-receiving and whom it will not be possible to distinguish with certainty. These people receive most of their income from purchases by state institutions or state employees. The latter is especially hard to be sure of. For instance, those working for *The Guardian* and *New Statesman & Society* might just fit this category. But if it is too hard to prove then they might have to be given the benefit of the doubt. Though if the state sector shrinks, due to a new Taxpayer Democracy, then enterprises will decline to the extent that they necessarily depend on indirect state patronage.

16) Civil Society and Civil Liberties: Two Statist Views Reviewed

(From the *Times Higher Educational Supplement*, March 3, 1995.)

Title: ***Conditions of Liberty: Civil Liberty and Its Rivals***
Author: Ernest Gellner
Reviewer: J. C. Lester
Publisher: Hamish Hamilton
ISBN: 0 241 00220 6
Pages: 225pp
Price: £18.99

Title: ***Liberty in Britain 1934 - 94: A Diamond Jubilee History of the National Council for Civil Liberties***
Author: Brian Dyson
Reviewer: J. C. Lester
Publisher: Civil Liberties Trust
ISBN: 0900 137 39 8
Pages: 100pp
Price: £6.99

I fill Ernest Gellner with disgust: disgust at my views and disgust at his inability to say exactly what is wrong with them (or so he once remarked in his social philosophy seminar). Gellner fills me with frustration. He is always penetrating, witty and erudite (except when using "egotism" for "egoism"), but I cannot see how his ideas from social anthropology can be a substitute for real philosophy and economics. His new book is no exception.

Gellner loves Civil Society—his capitals—rather than liberty; the subtitle of his book is more accurate than the title. Civil Society to him means the institutions that are a check upon the state while being protected by it. He thinks that Civil Society distinguishes liberal democracy from communism, and he contrasts it, illuminatingly, with primitive agrarian societies and Islamic states, both of which have no Civil Society but remain stable.

Like most people, Gellner thinks that communism in the USSR has recently ended. In fact it ended in 1921 when Lenin's attempt (under "War Communism") to abolish money—following Marx—failed. It is impossible to run an advanced industrial society by central planning and without money: the USSR was much more state-regulated, and so much less pluralistic, than the western democracies—but it remained an inegalitarian, commodity society with money, which was always economically inefficient. Gellner was taken in by Soviet prestige projects: forced and fruitless industrialisation, the space race, nuclear weapons.

The collapse of the USSR has liberated the desire for Civil Society and nationalism, especially the latter. And, according to Gellner, "modular man" is needed for both. "Modular man" with his "move from Status to Contract", is more or less free man, as Gellner more or less sees. So far so good. But nationalism, far from being in our interests, as Gellner supposes, is tribal atavism: the desire to be part of a community in order to fend off outsiders—with disastrous economic consequences.

Gellner assaults the "unconstrained" market with flaccid prejudices. It would "disrupt everything", he says, but we are not told how. Nor why the state must control the "social infrastructure", making, he admits, "lumpy and irreversible decisions" at a cost of half the subjects' incomes. Nor is it explained why insurance and charity could not replace state welfare. He thinks that liberty and economic efficiency often diverge in practice. This is because he mistakenly equates material growth with economic efficiency. But freer societies always produce more utility, and that is economic efficiency (as Shaw rightly put it, economics is about making the most of life). A related economic error is in thinking that "positional goods", things conferring relative status, are *ipso facto* finite and destructive of economic growth. It is normal to seek status in different ways, as Gellner sees, but these have different values, and are not "illusions". The market can indefinitely multiply ponds for each big fish that wants its own pond to swim in.

Is Civil Society really an "amoral order"? It has no religious backing, but surely "the liberty of the individual" can be a secular moral slogan? True, we cannot have "justifications" or "validations" of liberty—those who think we can are deluded, as Karl Popper has taught us.

Brian Dyson's *Liberty in Britain* is a concise, informative, and lively history of the National Council for Civil Liberties, or Liberty as it has been called since 1989. It shows that the NCCL has always had a left-wing bias, i.e., it has defended the liberty of the individual rather than that of the property owner. The NCCL has often sided with the unions in attacking the property-owning liberties of employers. The council was originally inspired by a desire to defend marchers from the use of *agents provocateurs* by the police. This aim was then codified as being "to resist all encroachments on our liberties". A noble purpose, but one that the NCCL has not always honoured.

It defended, with varying success, freedom of communication and assembly. But it was ambivalent, at best, about defending similar freedoms for fascist organisations and fascists. It supported Oswald Mosley's imprisonment without trial in wartime (though 39 members resigned), for instance, and it criticised the management of the Albert Hall for refusing to grant permission for anti-fascist meetings. It has never accepted that freedom of assembly can only be handled liberally by agreements between private groups wishing to hold meetings and private property owners. State control of the right to demonstrate in Oxford Street, Hyde Park, and so on, inevitably creates clashes between groups that cannot be resolved liberally. The same applies to the NCCL's views on the rights of travellers and gypsies.

To have one's choice of customers and employees dictated, on whatever basis, is as certain an attack on liberty as to have one's choice of friends and lovers dictated. The former is more of a 'property liberty' restriction though, and left-wing groups such as the NCCL support it. The NCCL does not see that compulsory integration is as illiberal as compulsory segregation, and the proximate cause of much violence. The NCCL's support for, *inter alia,* the Race Relations Act and the Race Relations Board was, therefore, an attack on liberty and welfare. However, in its campaigns to relax immigration controls the NCCL was more libertarian. For in this area the state restricts both the liberty of the individual (immigrants and potential immigrants) and the liberty of property owners (those who invite the immigrants). In general, though, the NCCL does not see that Liberty with a capital L must embrace both types of liberty.

17) Libertarian Controls on Guns, Drugs, Prostitution, Immigration, Etc., via Private Streets: How to be More Libertarian and Less Alarming than the No-Control Fetishists

(Libertarian Alliance online, 1996.)

Alarming and unlibertarian policies

It is often argued by libertarian types that there should be No Controls on this or that. The argument usually combines two factors: the supposed evidence that the controls are disastrous; and the supposed axiomatic fact that the repeal of state legislation must be more libertarian (though the latter point seems to oblige more-libertarian-than-thou types to 'stick to their guns' whatever the consequences). My chief contentions here are that many No Controllers are conceptually confused and that this confusion often causes them to argue for alarming and unlibertarian policies: policies that defend not liberty but licence; that is, having the power to infringe the liberty of others.

The market gives us anarchic controls, polycentrically achieved, rather than no controls at all. The libertarian solution to clashes in preferred controls is to allow people to choose to live in areas which operate their preferred rules, or to set up such areas if they do not already exist (by joining with like-minded people to buy up the land). This is libertarian because it is not done by aggressively imposing one's own preferences on other people.

Aggressively imposed tolerance

While the streets are owned by the state, it is impossible to opt out of whatever controls the state imposes on those streets. Moreover, the state *cannot* avoid imposing its own controls on many things, including guns, drugs, prostitution, and immigration. *Whatever* the state says about these matters, it will be aggressively imposing its Procrustean regulations on all the subjects in the country it occupies. Even if the state were to say that there are No Controls it would in reality be saying that it would *aggressively impose a tolerance* of all these things over its entire territory. Perhaps it would be more libertarian for the state to impose a universal tolerance of some of these things than for it universally to restrict them. But that would still only be a crude approximation to what the more libertarian market would have provided if left to itself. There would be no way that one could keep these things away from where one lives. This is the crucial point: *state-imposed tolerance is itself a state-control* and one that will impose on many people who would have opted out given a free-market, libertarian choice. It seems likely to me that, for instance, most parents of young children would prefer to opt for residential areas that restrict some of the above things. If so, then to impose the tolerance of them is to infringe the liberty of those parents.

The only *fully* libertarian position is to advocate that the state gets out of the way completely by privatising the streets, so that people can make their choices at the available competing prices. However, while the state does own the streets, there are at least less bad things that it can do. Libertarians should also want to be practical in the short term, for there will surely only be a series of practical short terms that leads to libertarianism (as there will not be a libertarian revolution in the violent sense, I believe and hope). So libertarians ought to suggest that the state at least tries to approximate to the market outcome, given that we can have some rough idea of what it is.

'Approximating to the market outcome' versus 'promoting the public interest'

It is often impossible to guess the market outcome. Is 'approximating to the market outcome' not hopelessly vague? Compared to the real market it is vague. But to opt for something like 'promoting the public interest' instead is precisely to drop the distinctively libertarian insight that it is market outcomes that are, apart from being libertarian, most likely to be in the public interest. 'Promoting the public interest' is so vague that every ideology that is not positively misanthropic, such as some Green extremism, can claim to be using it as a 'criterion'. It is about as nebulous as 'being guided by what is good'.

On certain issues the approximate market outcome is not so controversial. The market would certainly provide us with some, probably minimal, traffic rules for our safety and convenience. It would obviously be ridiculous to advocate No Traffic Control along the lines that a spontaneous order will evolve—though to be consistent the No Controllers ought to do this. Some kind of order would evolve, but it requires private property to evolve such rules *efficiently*. The common property that is effectively being advocated here is more likely to result in varieties of the 'tragedy of the commons'. Neither do No Controllers normally advocate that the state allow people to carry around nuclear bombs or to have them at home. These things are obviously too dangerous to the innocent.

The unclear consequences of repealing gun control

With some other issues the most libertarian state policy is often less clear. In the case of guns, the No Control fetishists do not always seem to know whether they would want them *no matter what* the consequences. But surely gun murders and maimings are themselves infringements of freedom. Whether the repeal of existing state legislation on guns would be more libertarian just depends on the consequences. When looking at the evidence, the consequences are far from clear to me. It is very hard to compare across cultures (the USA is hardly homogeneous itself) or times (as L P. Hartley wrote, "the past is another country"). Society in the UK has changed since the gentle times before the First World War when it was safe to allow guns to be completely legal. Imagine the road rage or football hooliganism we have today but with guns freely available. Society is simply much more violent today, partly thanks to the lack of serious punishments for violent crimes. Shotguns did have a fairly safe record when they were (relatively recently) banned in the UK, but surely it is handguns that are more tempting to carry around. Switzerland is full of guns still and reputedly safe (though I have heard this disputed), but then the Swiss are a highly law-abiding people who will not even cross an empty road until the crossing light allows them to do so. It might be more libertarian for the state to allow a little competitive variety, which would also approximate to the market in action to some degree, rather than to opt for any particular imposition. In a free market there would still be some areas where guns would almost certainly be available, such as in the countryside and at firing ranges.

Freedom writers rather than freedom fighters

One bizarre defence of imposing universal gun tolerance can be rejected more easily. This is the idea that libertarians will need guns either for some kind of libertarian revolution or to protect a libertarian anarchy from a reactionary statist takeover. As Etienne de La Boetie and David Hume clearly saw, the fundamental rules of society rest on public opinion. It is not possible for a handful of people with a few weapons to impose a fundamentally different social system than what the majority understand and want. That is why all reasonable libertarians are freedom writers rather than freedom fighters. We need to capture the hearts and minds of the majority to approach a stable society where market-anarchy has become common sense. (Though I do not intend by this to rule out the defiance of illiberal state commands on many issues.)

How to limit immigration

On the issue of immigration controls, the practical short-term solution seems highly problematic, at least to me. With fully private streets and without tax-funded handouts, a new and advantageous migration equilibrium would soon be established. The poor of the entire world would certainly not want to come to cold, rainy Britain. In the meantime, though it might be more libertarian on balance, it cannot fully be libertarian to abolish immigration controls while those who want to keep the potentially troublesome immigrants at a distance cannot do so. And while there are tax-funded handouts it is not clear whether it would be more libertarian to limit immigration or to allow it in the hope that it would undermine the system of handouts (I tend to favour the latter policy).

Voluntary segregation versus compulsory racial integration

By analogous argument, we do not need a nationwide curfew on the young, as one Labour MP recently suggested. But a lot of older people would be relieved to be able to move into areas where they knew that noisy youngsters, young thugs, etc., could legitimately be excluded. Sometimes people would be racially excluded. Compulsory racial integration, as currently imposed by the state, is possibly a greater evil than compulsory racial segregation: forcing people together when at least some of them would rather keep apart is more likely to result in violence. Voluntary segregation, thanks to private estates, is increasingly avoiding a lot of racial conflict in the USA. Such freedom of association is a basic civil liberty and not a privilege of any particular group. Fundamentalist Muslims can have areas that deny access to non-Muslims, or even enforce Islamic law, on this libertarian basis. Of course, none of these things is 'immigration control' in the nation-statist sense; but we might say that they are the libertarian translation and even extension of such control.

The superiority of voluntary solutions via private street control

Simply to repeal state legislation would, on many issues, be to impose the *contrary* unlibertarian error on everyone. In the cases under discussion, the general libertarian position must be to emphasise the superiority of voluntary solutions via private street controls, or at least of approximating to such a system. It is not libertarian to force people to put up with all manner of things they are highly concerned to avoid. That is authoritarian.

18) Anti-Libertarianism: a Book Review

(On *Anti-Libertarianism*, by Alan Haworth, *Journal of Applied Philosophy*, vol. 14, no. 1, 1997.)

In this book Alan Haworth tends to sneer at libertarians. However, there are, I believe, a few sound criticisms. I have always held similar opinions of Murray Rothbard's and Friedrich Hayek's definitions of liberty and coercion, Robert Nozick's account of natural rights, and Hayek's spontaneous-order arguments. I urge believers of these positions to read Haworth. But I don't personally know many libertarians who believe them (or who regard Hayek as a libertarian).

Perhaps the most useful response is to challenge some of Haworth's other views. He uses 'right-wing' to mean something like unregulated property matters. By analogy, I take 'left-wing' to mean unregulated personal matters. As libertarians want both areas unregulated they fit better on an unregulated-regulated axis, with extreme state regulation in both areas as an opposite. So the market is *not* the central tenet of libertarianism (contra p. 36). Libertarianism embraces all voluntary behaviour not imposing on others, including charity such as the Good Samaritan's (which example Haworth would twist to defend state intervention [pp. 100-103]).

Haworth denies that liberty is "'essentially' negative" (p. 47). But surely liberty is, analytically, about the *absence* of constraints. More precisely here, it is about people not being constrained by other people. To avoid confusion, I call this 'interpersonal liberty'. Hence falling into a pit does *not* reduce *interpersonal* liberty (contra p. 49) but being pushed in does, unless that is part of defence, restitution, or retribution (so it is false that "coercion and [interpersonal] liberty stand opposed" [contra p. 46]).

Though sometimes bad at expressing it, libertarians have a good grasp of interpersonal liberty as 'persons not (proactively) imposing on each other'. Such an account of liberty does not mention private property, though normal observance entails it. The market restricts one's *licence* (to impose) rather than certain (interpersonal) *liberties* (contra p. 54). Haworth's unseen trespassing child *does* impose (contra p. 97): by flouting the owner's choices, thus attacking liberty. By contrast, Haworth lacks any clear grasp of interpersonal liberty and hence libertarian acquisition, so cannot understand why state-expropriated utilities are illiberal (p. 10). He writes of "liberalism" as though ignorant of classical liberalism (p. 27) (and of the "true levellers" as though ignorant of the, libertarian, levellers [p. 10]). Perhaps that is why he sees no connection between liberty and the market.

Libertarians do not believe the market to be "the perfect moral order" (contra p. 3), merely better than state aggression. And lack of libertarian rights does not entail lack of moral obligation (contra pp. 78-9). To accept a right to liberty is not, *ipso facto*, to "confuse questions concerning rights with questions concerning freedom" (contra p. 11): following Karl Popper's epistemology, libertarians can simply conjecture the desirability of libertarian rights (viewing these as compatible with the market and utility, for conceptual and empirical reasons). Haworth writes nothing to refute this.

There are many completely unargued assertions. Exactly how does democracy respect choice better than the market (p. 17)? (If 'democratic' means to "facilitate self-determination for autonomous beings" [p. 102], then I guess the market is 'democratic'.) How are "huge capitalist corporations" not merely successful but "coercive" (p. 101)? How does so-called "equal opportunities legislation" protect "the property women hold in their persons" (p. 142 n. 4) rather than being female privilege?

Typical libertarian views, whether right or wrong, are unknown or ignored on many issues. Libertarians typically think that: people command ever better market wages by selling only their labour (contra p. 21); unemployment is due to state benefits (contra p. 99) and depressions to inflated money and state profligacy (contra p. 100); the state *undermines* public goods (contra p. 92) and equality (contra p. 131); extorted transfers will harm the poorest in the long term (contra p. 109); state medicine (contra pp. 82-4) and state education (contra p. 132) not only violate liberty but are more expensive and inferior.

Haworth misunderstands how states impose pollution and merely ignores market-justice arguments (p. 113). Nuclear waste would not be in free-market lakes (contra p. 111) because damaged third parties could sue using contingency fees (though choosing *some* pollution, as city-dwellers do, is hardly intolerable).

He even scores some clear own goals: it recently took New York's *state-licensing* to curtail ethnic hairdressing (contra p. 87); and voluntary discrimination (i.e., freedom of association) is not *state-imposed* segregation, which is what killed Bessie Smith (contra p. 140, n. 9).

Overall, this book contains too many of Haworth's prejudices and too little careful consideration of the relevant arguments.

19) Behind the Caricature: Reply to a Befuddled Author

(A reply to Alan Haworth's letter, *Journal of Applied Philosophy*, vol. 15, no. 3, 1998.)

The editors of the *Journal of Applied Philosophy* allowed Alan Haworth to reply[1] to my short review of his *Anti-Libertarianism*.[2] The editors would not allow me to respond to Haworth. Thanks to the openness of internet publication and the Libertarian Alliance website, this can now be rectified and Haworth's reply can no longer escape a public critical response.

Haworth begins by quoting himself in the same sort of sneering at libertarians that I had noted in the review: "self-styled libertarians ... acolytes ... truly elect" and goes on specifically to mention "the activities of such minority groups as the Libertarian Alliance" (but he sneers at every kind of libertarianism in his book, as far as I can see). He thinks he can keep his criticism mainstream and thus escape the charge that he has "missed the point". But we ought to be looking for the strongest form of a thesis to criticise, and when someone tries to help us we should be grateful and try to answer his arguments. Unfortunately, Haworth seems more interested in anti-libertarian propaganda. How can it be of any significance if it were only a "minority group" that has answers to his criticisms? But in fact he appears inexcusably, sometimes laughably, ignorant of most standard libertarian literature outside the few targets he takes to represent the mainstream.

I have, he states, written an "immoderate and misleading review". I happily embrace the charge of "immoderate". Haworth has certainly written a moderate book—at best. Is my review misleading? We shall see. Apparently he is even annoyed (as his tone and style shows, though he tries to save face by calling this "weary resignation") that I agree with some of his points about Hayek, Nozick and Rothbard and that I urge people to read his criticisms. How these specific agreements show my "complete inability to answer the greater part of [his] case" escapes me—and him. If he has any case that I have supposedly missed then what is stopping him from saying what it is? Despite my filling the rest of the review with critical points, Haworth charges me with being "bereft of rational argument" (by which he can only really mean that he is bereft of a reply to the arguments I gave). I "resort, instead, to manoeuvres ... [irrelevant sneer omitted] ... to deflect attention from the inadequacy of the libertarian case by changing the subject." We shall look at the cited cases, but I cannot help feeling that he is judging others by his own abysmal standards. If I genuinely wanted to deflect attention from weak arguments, why would I explicitly agree with some of his arguments? And if I wanted to avoid criticism, why would all my points be answers to arguments of his? It is also both bad manners and the *ad hominem* fallacy to impugn the honesty of a critic to avoid his arguments.

Haworth asserts that my stated conception of liberty is "*recherché*". He thinks this will have "a tenuous connection with the real meanings of 'freedom' and liberty'". But words do not have "real meanings" in any fixed sense. In any case, the basic idea of interpersonal liberty as people not proactively imposing on each other is at one with commonsense understanding. And I apply it quite simply and explicitly to a few points that Haworth makes, in an honest attempt to answer his points. But he refuses to reply to any of these. Even a poor attempt would be better than merely, irrelevantly and erroneously, supposing that my conception is too unusual to be worth replying to. Fortunately for Haworth, he can now read about the conception at length in *Escape from Leviathan*.

I am also charged with "trying to change the subject by taking [him] to task for not having said things which [sic] it would have been quite beside the point to say in any case." His sole example is that I supposedly criticized him for "not having paid close attention to the precise meaning of 'right-wing'." I did nothing of the kind. The meaning of words is nothing to do with solving serious intellectual problems. I was explaining how it is possible to add a North-South dimension to the Left-Right one[3] that helps to make it clear that—and *this* is the point—"the market is *not* the central tenet of libertarianism (contra p. 36). Libertarianism embraces all voluntary behaviour ..., including charity such as the Good Samaritan's (which example Haworth would twist to defend state intervention [pp. 100—103])." Is Haworth dishonestly evading this point or is he simply incapable of understanding it? (Note that this is not an *ad hominem*, for I am not using it as an excuse to dismiss or avoid his arguments—in the Haworthian style. Neither do I think it bad manners to give tit for tat.)

It *is* necessary for Haworth to explain how equal opportunities legislation is *not* female privilege (which point of mine he carefully omits) because it supposedly *protects* "the property women hold in their persons". For far from being an "uncontroversial assertion" I can make no sense of it: what have equal opportunities to do with self-ownership? So as it stands this is not merely a prejudice but a particularly bizarre one. In any case, one purpose for philosophy is to challenge assertions that are assumed to be "uncontroversial". (And I was not "alluding to a footnote" for I gave the full reference.)

I have recently noticed how bad arguers, when repeatedly charged with not answering a crucial point sometimes start referring to the point as a "mantra". This is a foolish attempt to excuse their inability to answer the point. Even if a phrase is repeated in a mantra-like fashion that does not make it false. Haworth objects thus that "Lester simply [I say nothing else, ever?] reiterates, but more insistently [how does he know it is more? What is wrong with that anyway?] the libertarian mantra according to which free market operations inevitably work to produce the general good". But, in fact, the nearest thing to this "mantra" appears only *once* where I say that libertarians can "conjecture the desirability of libertarian rights (viewing these as compatible with the market *and* utility....)". The next nearest thing to this point is where I make *specific* points to illustrate my assertion that "Typical libertarian views, *whether right or wrong*, are unknown or ignored on many issues" (emphasis added). My point is *not* to assert that the market is better for welfare as well as liberty, but that Haworth merely ignores specific libertarian lines of argument (which space limitations prevented me from doing more than mentioning) that this is so as though they do not exist. If Haworth were more familiar with the literature he would see that, whether he agrees with it or not, far from being "vulgar invisible-handism" it applies sophisticated economics and empirical research to explain how government failure is mistaken for market failure. It is *his* "naïve faith" in politics that is the problem. Though he will fool some others as well as himself, repeating the accusations of "vulgar invisible-handism" and "mantra" (in a mantra-like way, of course) cannot get him out of doing his homework.[4]

Haworth's final point is that I caricature what he says by exaggerating it. His first example (I quote Haworth properly rather than engage in muddled or mendacious paraphrase): "I did not confidently assert that democracy respects choice better than the market—only that 'Imperfect though these [democratic procedures] may be, there is no need to swallow the improbable libertarian myth.' That the former are necessarily much worse at respecting choice than the latter." Here Haworth is going out of his way to make a fool of himself by doing the very thing of which he falsely accuses me. I write nothing like "confidently assert". I merely asked, "Exactly how does democracy respect choice better than the market (p. 17)?" Presumably he does mistakenly think it does so at least *sometimes*, or he would not be writing the book. Why does he not give one example or explanation rather than dismissing the libertarian position without considering it?

And again: "Nor, as Lester claims, did I deny that 'liberty is, analytically, about the absence of constraints.' On the contrary, I *assert* just that, adding only that the claim, though true, is 'tautologically vacuous' [p. 44]" First, Haworth does not assert that 'liberty is, *analytically*, about the absence of constraints' even on page 44, a different page from the one I was quoting from. He writes only that, "the claim that freedom is merely the absence of *constraint* ... might seem tautologically uninformative." He does not even paraphrase or quote himself accurately and honestly here. But I did not claim that he denied this. What I actually wrote is, "Haworth denies that liberty is '"essentially" negative (p. 47)". Now, "denies" is strictly shorthand for the *precise* way that he rejects the idea. But that is irrelevant anyway. For I made my assertion mainly as part of my explanation of the fairly ordinary libertarian conception of liberty: "people not being constrained by other people". He has dismissed this simple explanation as "*recherché*" without criticising it or its applications to what he says. When he goes on that "Lester clearly hasn't grasped what I have to say on the subject of Freedom" this is more irony, as his own conception is certainly "*recherché*" as well as a hopeless muddle.

This same backfiring accusation continues with Haworth's assertion that "Lester would have liked to portray me as just another 'loony lefty' trotting out some fairly tired sub-Marxist clichés." I never stated or implied anything like this. In fact, I was not trying to portray Alan Haworth in any way whatsoever. I have no interest in Mr Haworth. This is not personal (for me, at least). I was discussing the objective arguments in his book. I was agreeing with what I thought was right in the book and making explicit what I disagreed with, and why, as best I could in the very limited space allocated by the editors.

Haworth is "quite unimpressed by Lester's *ex cathedra* remarks on 'what libertarians say'." It is not difficult to have more authority than Haworth on the subject of libertarianism. What a pity he did not show a draft of his book to a few libertarian academics. They would surely have steered him towards the relevant literature of which he is so woefully ignorant. It is not that my "brand of libertarianism is so 'pure', so squeaky clean, that [I] am not even prepared to count Hayek as a libertarian." It is that Haworth paints a picture of libertarians as typically endorsing sundry obnoxious social outcomes, when the most cursory survey of the academic libertarian literature should have corrected this view. Even if Hayek's libertarian credentials were not a matter of serious dispute (he is nowhere near being even a minimal statist), that would not in any way excuse Haworth's glaring errors of omission (which he ignorantly assumes to be "the arcane speculations in which the initiates of this or that navel-gazing *coterie* are liable to engage"). Rather than "examine the foundations of a doctrine which [sic] has proven largely influential in the real world" his few high-profile targets and his own ignorant assumptions about 'what libertarians think' mean he has mainly tackled something that is little better than a crude popular caricature.

Haworth has presented no sound argument that his book has been misrepresented in any way. State interference with education is at its worst when it allows people to pursue their propaganda hobbies in tax-funded posts.[5]

Notes

[1] *Journal of Applied Philosophy*, vol. 15, no. 3, 1998.
[2] *Journal of Applied Philosophy*, vol. 14, no. 1, 1997.
[3] http://www.la-articles.org.uk/pc.htm
[4] Haworth might like to start this on the Laissez-Faire Books website: http://www.laissezfairebooks.com/
[5] http://www.la-articles.org.uk/tax.htm

20) Right to Roam or Licence to Trespass?

(First published as a book chapter in *Another Country*, 1999.)

The 'right to roam' open and uncultivated countryside is a campaign that is gaining pace and that seems set to become legislation sooner or later. This would be immoral folly. I have no objection to roaming, or rambling, as such—as long as it is not compulsory either to roam or to suffer roamers. As the health fascists are slightly less influential than the egalitarians, the arguments in favour of making it compulsory to suffer roamers are making greater headway.

A brief outline of the case for a 'right to roam'

Arguments for the 'right to roam' the countryside certainly have a great deal of common sense on their side. They are not thereby mistaken, of course, though that fact should alert the sceptical intellect. Let me first outline the general case for the 'right to roam', as put across by advocates in the mass media, the Ramblers' Association, politicians, and one government department.

The great landowners of England did not create the land that they own. These landowners are often personally rich and merely being selfish killjoys by denying others access to such natural beauty ("Access to this part of our common heritage is something which should be enjoyed by the many, not the few"[1]). They have often inherited their land from ancestors who themselves had a dubious claim to it. If they bought land with this as a background, then that does not make much difference. In any case, "individuals may hold the legal title, but really the land is owned by us all."[2] So we should be able to roam all over any uncultivated parts, even away from any traditional public footpaths. Ramblers should not have to pay the landowners and neither should the landowners normally be compensated for this in any way (such as by tax relief). There should also be facilities for the disabled as far as this is practical. The overall result will be that "access to the open countryside will make a significant contribution to improving public health and reducing social divisions …."[3]

Why these arguments are wrong

In all this there is little substantial argument, mainly mere presumption and whimsy. It is a combination of egalitarian bigotry and irrelevant pro-health waffle. But, if only for the enlightenment of the elected oligarchs who might impose this 'right' on us, let us now consider this 'roamish' propaganda in a little more detail.

There are oft-repeated arguments putting forward the health virtues of rambling. But all these are irrelevant unless there is no other way for people to be healthy and no way that land access could be voluntary. These two possibilities are patently not the case. So these health arguments can simply be put aside immediately. The great landowners of England often did and do, to varying extents, create what is worth enjoying about the land that they own. The land is not always in a natural state, but is often well developed and maintained. Without the owners there would often be no easy movement across the land or views to see. That the landowners are often personally rich cannot itself be a reason for imposing on them. Or if it is, then there needs to be some independent argument concerning this rather than just an appeal to envious Procrusteanism.

Ramblers should not expect their leisure activity to be free

Neither is there any reason to think that the landowners exclude people from their land for no good reason. There is no way that having indefinite numbers of people walking across their land cannot impose costs on the owners in terms of physical damage and loss of privacy (owners regularly attest to both). Perhaps it is not usually as bad from a privacy viewpoint as having people walk around your back garden without your permission, but the general principle is the same and the financial losses through damage can certainly be far higher.

Once this elementary point is grasped, one can see that if people are not prepared to pay the landowners the price that those owners would set for access to their land, then that is good evidence that the would-be roamers are simply imposing a cost in excess of any value that they will receive from their roaming. The only way to be fairly sure we are avoiding this is for the roamers freely to negotiate to buy or rent any right of way or general access that they choose. Instead, the roamers want to enjoy their pursuits at other people's imposed expense. This is likely to have a negative-sum result, in broadly utilitarian terms. Hence it is anti-social. Roamers think they can get away with this because the owners are generally an unpopular minority—the 'rich'—whose interests it is politically safe to discount. Like anti-fox hunting, the 'right to roam' has no serious case. The anti-fox hunters do not offer a more humane alternative to hunting the pest (shooting and poisoning it would clearly be worse), and they usually turn a blind eye to the suffering the fox itself inflicts on other small mammals. They also often perceive members of the hunt as being from despised 'privileged' (really, advantaged) backgrounds. The 'right to roam' similarly includes some combination of superficial sentiment about 'nature' and malicious political classism (which seems no more defensible than political racism or sexism—as opposed to private discrimination or freedom of association).

If an existing owner's claims to the land are in any way dubious, then that is a good reason to present a detailed case on an individual basis and to challenge the property claims in the courts. If successful, the property should then be returned to the legitimate owners. The existence of a few dubious property claims is not a good reason to introduce an indiscriminate licence to trespass.

What the 'roamers' are demanding is a licence to trespass, not a 'right to roam'

Why do I call this 'licence'? Because there is a crucial distinction between liberty and licence. In the social sense, 'liberty' means, roughly, not being interfered with by others in your person and property. 'Licence' means, roughly, interfering with the person or property of others—such as walking across someone's land against his wishes. But how, it might be asked, can it be 'trespass' if the state allows it? For two reasons. First, assuming that the land is legitimately owned, the interference is objective whether it is allowed by the state or not. Secondly, state legislation allowing such roaming would only be lawful if the command (or 'big stick') theory of law were correct. And if that theory were correct then everything that the Nazis did, for instance, must be held to be perfectly lawful. But I don't see that the 'law' is simply whatever rules people with power can impose on others. Laws are primarily spontaneous social rules that have evolved for the common good; state legislation is conceptually dependent on, and corrupting of, these laws. However, these philosophical waters are too deep to enter into seriously here.

Reasonable libertarian rights of movement must require that there be some pathways through some properties where the owner would otherwise be being a mere obstacle to the free movement of other people. A very clear case of this would be if someone were to buy a thin strip of land with no other intention than to start charging a toll without adding any service. But such necessary rights of movement are few and far between in the cases under consideration. They are not what the 'roamers' are normally claiming.

If landowners charged for access, 'roamers' would also benefit

Once we understand the great general social value of exclusive property rights, we should be very reluctant to ride roughshod over such rights in any particular case without very strong reason (David Hume's *Enquiry Concerning the Principles of Morals*, 1751, is a good exposition of the social utility of private property). We should be especially reluctant when there is a clearly efficient voluntary alternative, as there is here: simply allowing the landowners to charge for and regulate access to their property. The landowners are unlikely to be able to charge very much, given that the service is hardly essential. They are unlikely to refuse altogether provided that people are prepared to pay a price that covers their costs. The landowners might even improve the facilities (maps, guides, toilets, cafes, ...) and advertise. Thus no one will be imposed on and both sides to the trade will gain (as is normal with all trade).

Contrary to activists' claims, the disabled are not a special case

As they are often mentioned—such as in the DETR consultation paper *Access to the Open Countryside in England and Wales*—what about the disabled? Those who are truly disabled are rightly objects of our compassion and, sometimes, charity. But to allow them to impose claims against innocent people is to turn them into social parasites who will eventually risk becoming despised—if they are not already becoming so. There is usually no amount of money that can compensate people for severe disabilities. Does this mean that they must be given rights to ever more of what others possess? Taken to its extreme, there is no stopping point short of the enslavement of the able by the disabled (even this might not be enough compensation to achieve equality of welfare). And every step on the way towards this is both immoral and inefficient. With the 'right to roam', as elsewhere, the seriously disabled should only be helped charitably—where the market will not suffice—if we are to avoid this additional egalitarian disaster. That the recipients often resent charity is a social boon and a spur to maintain independence; the 'welfare rights' the state gives foster both arrogance and dependence.

The problem is not lack of access, but excess of publicly owned land

In fact, we can go much further in our rejection of this bogus 'right to roam'. Far from allowing a 'right to roam' on private properties, we should do the exact opposite of what these 'rambler communists' are advocating. We should positively add to private property wherever this is possible. All those state-owned properties that currently allow unrestricted access should be sold off so that these resources can also be properly husbanded: maintained and developed, instead of being stuck in a 'tragedy of the commons' (where all have only an incentive to overuse). What of all the existing heaths and parks that are neglectfully owned by the state, or local authorities, for the reckless use of all? These should be sold or given away forthwith to private individuals, charitable trusts, or businesses, so that they can be added to the social efficiency that only private property and the market can generate. But much so-called private property is, in any case, so hedged about with state regulations that the putative owners' property claims are severely compromised. So these regulations must also be abolished.

It might be suggested that at least some public right to access, such as public footpaths, would seem to come traditionally and legitimately with the ownership of some land. However, that also seems to be an argument for some form of common ownership (though imposing worst on the landowner), which, similarly, cannot really improve liberty or welfare. It would be better if some people were allowed to own these rights privately, though that could always be through a charitable trust.

Activists fail to grasp basic economic concepts

Like most political problems, the main source of error here is a lack of understanding of basic economics and property concepts. This lack, though, is often shared by professors of economics, who reject the implications of free-market economics just because they are 'too extreme'—that is to say, counter to common sense. The solution will only be found in educating people about the economics and about the philosophical inadequacy of some common sense. Any discussion of 'rights' that does not have economic and philosophical clarification as a background, is likely to generate more heat than light.

Under no circumstances should the absurd 'right to roam' be incorporated into the legislation of this country. In reality, it is clearly a mere licence to trespass. Armed with the appropriate economic and philosophical arguments, we should eventually be able to offer an effective counter-attack with a movement for the 'right to own' privately every last one of the state-controlled commons, heaths, hills, mountains, downs, woodlands, rivers, beaches, and footpaths. As a result, there will be no imposition on legitimate landowners and more access to better resources for ramblers.

Notes

[1] Dept of the Environment, Transport & the Regions (Welsh Office), *Access to the Open Countryside in England & Wales*, a consultation paper, p. 28.
[2] *Hansard*, 30 January 1998, col. 696.
[3] Dept of Environment, op. cit., p22.

General References

Access Campaign Bulletin, Issue 9, March 1998.
Freedom to Roam Factsheet, Ramblers Association, 1997.
Freedom with Responsibility, Rambling Today, Supplement, Spring 1996.

21) The Disability Studies Industry[1]

(From a commissioned report for the Social Affairs Unit, 2002.)

Introduction

This brief monograph was written in an attempt to discover the general situation of Disability Studies, given that this appears to have become a growth area in academia with various typically illiberal aspects. The findings bear out the initial impression. There is a style of argument, even propaganda (for there is usually little genuine engagement with opposing liberal views), that can be seen in many other areas of academia. It amounts to a relatively new 'progressive' industry with various fashionable keywords, phrases and ideologies—often not obviously related to disabilities in any serious way—indicating the nature of the beast: 'progressive', 'radical', 'oppression', 'bourgeois', 'empowerment', 'rights', 'equal opportunities', 'discrimination', 'prejudice', 'citizenship', 'social justice', 'socially constructed', 'Marxism', 'Post Modernism' and 'Feminism'. The overall picture is that disability has become increasingly politicised along politically correct lines to the detriment of society as a whole and, eventually, even to the disabled themselves. This is largely caused by the endemic *trahison des clercs* in our tax-consuming[2] and coercively monopolised university system.

The political approach is quite overt and even relished:

> The exciting thing about disability studies is that it is both an academic field of enquiry and an area of political activity ... involving the classrooms, the workplace, the courts, the legislature, the media, and so on. [Davis, 1997, 1]

This is typically linked to 'rights' and 'citizenship':

> ...in the United Kingdom the evidence that disabled people are still denied their full rights to citizenship is overwhelming. [Johnstone, 2001, 24]

And underpinning these 'rights' is usually the modern leftwing battle cry of 'social justice':

> Social justice is at the heart of disability theory and changing morality in the Western world. [Johnstone, 2001, 73]

The arguments

A main argument in the Disability Studies literature is that 'disability' is socially constructed, often for sinister (bourgeois) class reasons, rather than objective:

> That disablement is a socially constructed concept in the service and shaping of power is now a generally accepted orthodoxy. [Johnstone, 2001, 164]

The idea is to turn the tables by explaining how markets and industrialisation are the real problem rather than those labelled as disabled:

> ... the 'problem' is not the person with disabilities; the problem is the way that normalcy is constructed to create the 'problem' of the disabled person. ... the social process of disabling arrived with industrialisation. [Davis, 1997, 9]

The idea of what is normal is supposed to be some kind of bourgeois conspiracy:

> ... the very term that permeates our contemporary life—the normal—is a configuration that arises in a particular historical moment. It is part of a notion of progress, of industrialisation, and of ideological consolidation of the power of the bourgeoisie. [Davis, 1997, 28]

And so 'disability' has no objective meaning:

> At the heart of disability studies is a recognition that disability is a cultural construction; that is, that 'disability' has no inherent meaning. [Davis, 1997, 29]

Disability is thus supposed to be at least on a par with gender in its social construction or possibly even race, the two main areas that lead the way in this kind of argument and industry (in fact, all three are usually physical with race and sex largely genetic):

> Disability is not a biological given; like gender, it is socially constructed from biological reality. [Davis, 1997, 260]

Tendentious politicised definitions sometimes replace any serious attempt at argument:

> *Disability* The disadvantage or restriction of activity caused by a contemporary social organisation which takes no or little account of people who have physical impairments and thus excludes them

from participation in the mainstream of social activities. (UPIAS, 1976: pp. 3-4) [Quoted in Barnes, 1999, 28]

Contra the complaints about industrialisation somehow manufacturing 'disability', it is mainly the market that has eliminated a vast amount of disability through increased wealth and advances in medical sciences (which go hand in hand). Thus, polio and tuberculosis are things of the past. Where disabilities remain, things like electric wheelchairs and pain-killing drugs make life much easier for the disabled. But there is a grain of, vacuous, truth in the 'social construction' claim. It is logically necessary that if every aspect of everyday life were provided with full facilities to counterbalance every aspect of every type of disability (or 'impairments', as the latest PC approach now prefers to put it[3]) then the disabled would, of course, be able to do everything that everyone else does. In this sense, people are only 'disabled' by an environment that does not fully compensate for their incapacities. But how relevant is this *a priori* point? It stubbornly ignores three obvious things: 1) the fact that a disability needs to be compensated for shows that it is an objective disadvantage, and it is mere PC Speak to deny it; 2) the unimaginably vast expense of creating such a logical possibility as universal compensating facilities for each impairment; 3) that this vast expense, or even any degree of movement towards it, must be at the proactively imposed expense of other people (to the extent that it is not paid for voluntarily, which must be relatively limited).

A second, related, main argument—often bound up with the first—is that the disabled are an oppressed group but, unlike women and non-white races, one not yet generally recognised as being so even among 'progressives':

> Progressives in and out of academia may pride themselves on being sensitive to race or gender, but they have been 'ableist' in dealing with the issue of disability. [Davis, 1997, 1]

And so the main problems are the similar ones of 'prejudice' and 'discrimination':

> ...disabled men and women have been subject to the same form of prejudice, discrimination and segregation imposed upon other oppressed groups ... on the basis of characteristics such as race or ethnicity, gender, and aging. [Davis, 1997, 174]

But genuine oppression surely involves such *proactive* impositions as persecution, enslavement, and expropriation. What Disabilities Studies regards as 'oppression' is merely failing to provide the full benefits of opportunities completely equal to the non-disabled.[4] And proactively to impose the costs of this provision to any degree, as they advocate, would itself be—and is now, in fact—an oppression of the able for the benefit of the disabled and the growing numbers of those employed in the Disability Industry (it might be enlightening to know what percentage of what is spent actually reaches the disabled themselves). Ironically, the 'helpers' of the disabled can actually oppress their clients in all sorts of ways from bullying to bossing them about: (These are examples of the two groups that live at the taxpayers' expense: the underclass, that the disabled are pushed into, and the professional overclass, that 'look after them'.)

These two general arguments, about the supposed social construction and oppression of the disabled, are applied to all the various areas of disability *mutatis mutandis*. However, the hearing impaired include a particularly vociferous vanguard interest group who wish to affirm their difference as some kind of 'equally valid lifestyle' that is mainly inconvenienced by the attitudes of others. They are not really disabled at all but an oppressed "linguistic community":

> Nowadays, two constructions of deafness in particular are dominant and compete for shaping deaf peoples' destinies. The one construes deaf as a category of disability; the other construes deaf as designating a member of a linguistic community. [Davis, 1997, 154].

With disabilities generally, though,

> The Disability Rights Movement has shifted the construct of disability 'off the body and into the interface between people with impairments and socially disabling conditions' [Davis, 1997, 154]

Thus all disabilities tend to form a politicised interest group that is increasingly moving away from the traditional idea of seeking voluntary help for those in genuine and deserving need and towards blaming 'society' for their lack of complete equality and demanding their 'rights' to this.

The ideological context of the arguments

These arguments are primarily informed by a view of the state as enabling or, as they often say, 'empowering'[5] without looking too hard, if at all, at those at whose imposed expense all this is supposed to take place. This is a standard anti-liberal argument that is called some variety of socialism, notably Marxism, in modern times (but which also goes back at least to the pre-Socratics in various forms). Some still cite aspects of Marxism to explain why disability is 'created':

> Clearly the process of industrialisation under capitalism is a major factor that has contributed to the prevalence of disability ... Central to this approach is what Marx called 'the industrial reserve army'. [Davis, 1997, 172]

As mentioned, 'Social justice' in some socialist sense is the main modern ideology to which they now appeal; but usually in a more Marxian than Rawlsian version—to which they object:

> The concept of social justice as a mutual consensus and cooperation in equal shares of any collective surplus managed by the state, is changed—to a perception of social justice as individual entitlement ... from right-wing political thinkers in the United States (e.g. Rawls 1971) .... [Johnstone, 2001, p. 158][6]

But these arguments have also been influenced by Post Modernist gobbledegook and other 'radical' philosophies:

> ... the person with disabilities will become the ultimate example, the universal image, the modality through whose knowing the postmodern subject can theorize and act. [Davis, 1997, 8]

> Particular interest lies in the impact of recent sociological debates, notably social constructionism and feminism, as well as the suggested shift towards a postmodern society. [Barnes, 1999, 37]

> Radical theories—Marxism, feminism (as examples) and the like—offer a more constructive model for disabled politics because they seek to transform society and conceive liberty, rights and freedoms as socially constructed—rather than individually based—and socially denied by the exercise of power and oppression. [Johnstone, 2001, 103]

The impact of the arguments

The primary impact of these arguments is intellectual and on other academics, social workers, students and the vocal disabled themselves. But to be effective the secondary intellectual impact must be on the politicians, the ruling class, who will have to be converted in order to bring about any desired changes. Ultimately, of course, ordinary members of the public will be forced to bear the real cost of these various things.

One relatively recent example of proposed legislation seems to epitomise the problem. This was that all new houses must be built without doorsteps and have such things as wide enough halls and doorways to accommodate wheelchairs just in case a disabled person might want to live there or merely even visit (as it 'discriminates against' wheelchair users otherwise). But doorsteps serve a useful function in keeping out water and dirt. And the extra expense of wider spaces means that it might be cheaper simply to build every wheelchair user a free house wherever he wants it. But as that might look too obviously like an absurd privilege, we are lumbered with the even greater overall expense. And universal wheelchair access to all buildings, which we seem to be rapidly approaching, is considerably more diseconomic (insofar as it is not a voluntary affair).[7] According to Mindspring this has now become law:

> In March '98, Parliament passed the mandate ... Among the requirements are an accessible approach to the dwelling, a zero-step entrance when topography permits, at least a half-bath on the main floor, wide halls and doorways and accessible switches and electrical outlets.
> http://concretechange.home.mindspring.com/uknews.htm[8]

It would be possible to produce an economic analysis of the diseconomies of every single aspect of what the Disability Studies industry demands. They sometimes vaguely recognise the need for economy, but the best they can usually offer is that the disabled would be more likely to be productively employed rather than on state benefits (at what cost, they do not try to calculate). In any case, it is an axiom for the industry that 'social justice' trumps mere 'bourgeois' economics.

Opposition to the arguments

There is not much obvious published opposition to this output. On the shelves of bookshops under Disability Studies, in particular, there is next to nothing. The usual Public Choice theory applies. There is no tax-money to be gleaned by opposing the appropriation of tax-money by others. But there is tax-money to be shared in joining them or campaigning for an alternative tax-consuming project. There is also the additional factor here that anyone questioning such arguments might appear particularly heartless and, especially in statist academia, possibly risk ostracism and professional difficulties. At the extreme, the opposition are sometimes even hysterically accused of Nazi eugenics and a form of attempted 'genocide' of the disabled, especially when the opposition suggests that—completely voluntary—genetics and abortions can help minimise undesirable disabilities:

Our present situation connects with the Nazi past in that once again scientists and physicians are making the decisions about what lives to 'target' as not worth living by deciding which tests to develop. [Davis, 1997, 200]

The interests involved

The academics, social workers and disabled form a loose interest group of sorts, but with significant differences of interest, along Public Choice Theory lines. Behind the apparently scholarly and moral debate is often the bottom line of 'more resources' (tax-funding) for this or that activity. With academics and social workers there is more interest in 'empire building' for themselves: more professionals with more control of more resources. The vocal disabled often express a desire to take more direct control of services and resources. In this they are competing with those officially employed to make these decisions: "…if disability groups can organise themselves effectively there is an opportunity for disabled people to be collectively in control of the services they receive for the first time." [Hales, 1999, 95] However, it is unrealistic to overlook the active role of idealism in all this. In nearly every case this will be a bigger factor than financial interest. And many are just bored so actively look around for causes to champion.

The numbers of asserted disabled is enormous and questionable. Is it really plausible that as many as 15% in the US are disabled in any serious sense? [Davis, 1997, 1] 20% of the working population in the UK are disabled according to the Disability Rights Commission (Disability Briefing: February 2001). One in five is remarkably high. Is it mere cynicism to think that these figures might be inflated by various special interests, combined with lenient testing of such claims?

Views of the disabled

Quite a few of the academics prominently involved in Disability Studies are themselves in one or more of the disabled groups. Many of the vocal disabled use the arguments in more popular literature, including newsletters. There is a current campaign slogan implicitly designed to politicise the disabled: 'nothing about us, without us.' Though ostensibly a modest demand that the disabled be heard, what this really amounts to is a demand that the disabled have some political influence in any decision that might affect them in any way whatsoever (rather as 'stakeholder theory', with respect to business activities, also attempts to do):

> ... there is a need for much stronger statutory underpinning of consultation, with enforceable legal rights for disabled people. [Hales, 1996, 17]

> These would include comprehensive anti-discrimination laws ... and the appropriate resourcing of the nationwide network of organisations controlled and run by disabled people to ensure their implementation. [Hales, 1996, 44]

There is also now Disability Awareness Training, as 'awareness training' has long existed for race and 'gender'. This embodies the idea that, "negative attitudes underpin discrimination against disabled people." [Hales, 1996, 121] That discrimination in employment might be entirely rational, economic and a liberal right is rarely considered. But Disability Equality Training goes even further, with,

> its routes in the struggles of disabled people to gain equal opportunities and social justice. Disability Equality Training is primarily about changing the meaning of disability from individual tragedy to social oppression ... and the links with other oppressed groups. [Hales, 1996, 121]

On the other hand, we have the likes of Evelyn Glennie, the famous percussionist, who does her best to fit in with normal life despite her deafness without making a fuss or wishing to impose on others. Her championing of this attitude has made her something of a *bête noire* among the disability lobby.

However, the average disabled person is probably no more politicised or vocal than the average, politically apathetic person. Despite this, they will not be indifferent to voting for the candidate who promises them things at others' imposed expense: the form of vote-buying that is not merely legal but inherent to representative democracy.

The impact on medicine

There appears to be something of a power struggle between the medical profession, broadly conceived, and academics, particularly sociologists and political scientists but there are now some who are explicitly Disability Studies specialists. The medical professions, though they have their own Public Choice agenda to some extent, tend to want to treat the disabled to give them as normal a life as possible. The academics tend to wish to politicise the debate—disputing the very idea of what is 'normal', as we have seen—and seek more 'resources' and 'rights'. As the academics are more or less professional arguers with an armoury of 'isms' and more of a specific interest group with respect to this issue, they seem to be getting the better of the medical profession and this is likely to continue. At times this must appear to the layman to go beyond parody:

> Feminists have been challenging medicine's authority for many years now ... I look forward to the development of a full feminist theory of disability. [Davis, 1997, 275]

A particular problem is that cures and even ameliorations for various disabilities are seen as threats by those who see the attitudes of society as the problem—and maybe who want to protect their own empires. The laudable medical aim of reducing or eradicating various disabilities in various liberal ways, including entirely voluntary genetics and abortions, is sometimes opposed by disability groups:

> The disability rights agenda opposes genetic diagnosis on the grounds that it devalues the lives of disabled people. [Johnstone, 2001, 89][9]

> ...genetic testing is a form of contemporary barbarism to which society has not yet awoken... [Johnstone, 2001, 89]

At their most extreme, they even seem to want to increase the population of those who are similarly disabled. A recent case is the deaf lesbian couple that sought to maximise the chances of having a deaf child, by insemination from a deaf man. Setting aside whether this might leave the child with a legal claim against the parents for intentional harm, why should he ever receive any subsidies from taxation for what was entirely deliberate and not even perceived as undesirable?

Possible future areas of research, conferences, and publications

Perhaps it would be a useful corrective to attempt some anti-Disability Studies in the form of research, conferences and publications explicitly criticising Disability Studies as it currently exists. In responding to Disability Studies, the medical professions are the natural allies of the intellectual opposition and their voices would have authority with both politicians and the public. They also have 'common sense' on their side. Of course, one should not rule out involving economists, philosophers, etc., and the disabled themselves (especially when they are economists, philosophers, etc.).

In addition to some general and much needed anti-Disability Studies research, here are three specific research proposals to tackle the problem.

1. One radical alternative approach is to produce a report arguing that it is possible to encourage people to take out proper private insurance; both for themselves and their children should they become disabled and possibly for their unborn offspring should they be born disabled (insurance would be higher if one declines or fails a genetic test). It ought to be possible to show that it is quite likely that the disabled will end up having a better deal than they currently do. After all, it is now generally recognised that pensions would have been significantly higher if the money supposedly taken for so-called National Insurance (really a tax on employing people) were properly invested like a real insurance scheme instead of being spent by the government so that later taxpayers bear the burden of state pensions. Even if this were a compulsory scheme, that would be an improvement. Such an approach could be phased in to ensure that no currently disabled are left without support.

2. Produce detailed calculations of the vast expense that the bureaucracy of managing disability costs, along with the expense of such things as universal wheelchair access, and then argue that we should instead offer the disabled more direct cash—but at a tax-saving, obviously—to spend as they wish. This might have significant support from the disabled themselves, whose opinions certainly ought to count for more than those in the Disability Industry who wish to 'administer' and 'help' them. Having seen how relatively inexpensive this ought to be, an eventual move back towards voluntary, charitable, provision of genuinely deserving cases might then become much more practical (or at least phasing in such a thing as far as politics allows).

3. More generally, there could be a well-argued attack on the coercively monopolised and tax-subsidised university system. This should show how it could efficiently be physically de-politicised (no imposed monopoly, no tax-money) so that its employees are more likely to become ideologically de-politicised. Fully free-market institutions tend to be pro-market. It will just take time to get rid of the old guard. This should help to destroy the source of much of the illiberalism that is generating all these various industries (and vast amounts of general anti-liberal propaganda besides, which is influencing the wider society as well as corrupting the minds of so many young people who will become tomorrow's decision makers). A Public Choice School analysis of the various vested interests could be included.

Conclusion

Thanks mainly to the free market, the (dwindling proportion of the) objectively disabled have never had it so good. But this initial survey indicates the politically imposed harm that is currently occurring and the greater harm that is due. The very idea of Disability Studies ought not to presuppose that there is an 'oppressed' group that needs to be 'empowered' with its 'rights', though one could be forgiven for thinking this on looking through the mainstream literature. The severely disabled are rightly sympathised with and helped on a voluntary basis. The idea that any degree of disability gives you the automatic moral or legal right to compensation to bring you up to some normal level of welfare[10] is both impracticable and immoral. It also creates perverse incentives and moral hazards that inflate the numbers of the 'disabled' in a variety of ways. With ever more rights to be included at others' imposed expense, and rights to things paid for with other people's money, the disabled are in danger of being changed from the proper object of decent voluntary help, where there is genuine need, into a privileged and growing interest group of oppressors of more ordinary people—who will rightly regard them with a certain scepticism, at the very least.

Notes

[1] The original version of this paper was commissioned as a report with set headings and style of approach. Thus it is not how I would otherwise have written it and might read somewhat awkwardly in places. But rather than beginning afresh, which would be time-consuming, or abandoning a piece that seems to say something not said elsewhere, which is a contribution to the debate even if it were entirely mistaken, I present it more or less as I finally submitted it.
[2] This tax-consumption is on balance, or net, even where universities might also have substantial non-tax funding as well—such as the Open University. That academics are not (net) taxpayers but always tax consumers, cannot but influence their attitudes to calling for more 'resources' (tax funding). [http://212.67.202.149/~articles/tax.htm]
[3] But why stop at the possibly denigrating idea of 'impairments'? They might yet go on to assert that they are not even objectively impaired but merely different. For which differences are impairing depends on the social and technological conditions.
[4] It sometimes clarifies matters to consider these things at a personal level. Taking this conception seriously, one would apparently be actively 'oppressing' (all?) disabled people if one were biased in favour of marrying an able-bodied person.
[5] An irony that is clearly unintended here is that such 'empowering' is indeed an illiberal power over other people, proactively to force them to fund and accept the disabled/impaired/different. It is, then, a licence rather than a liberty they seek.

[6] Apparently Rawls's views on coercive redistribution to help the worst-off group are 'right-wing'—compared to these academics at least.
[7] It also leaves the country wide open to Dalek invasion, of course [this was written before the new flying Daleks].
[8] I cannot locate a more definite reference for the relevant legislation, but the main point is that this is the sort of diseconomic thing we have and that we can increasingly expect.
[9] Unless, perhaps (see the next paragraph), it is deliberately used to create a disabled person.
[10] Cf. Ronald Dworkin and Will Kymlicka, passim, extending John Rawls's arguments on Social Justice.

Bibliographical references

There is a plethora of books on Disability Studies. It might be possible to compile a bibliography of recent books alone as long as this article. I have mainly restricted myself to quoting from the following four books, as these appear to be in every way typical of the literature in the area while offering a broad selection of writers (though I have always cited them by the first editor or contributor), disabilities dealt with and academic disciplines.

Barnes, C., Mercer, G. & Shakespeare, T. (1999) *Exploring Disability: A Sociological Introduction*, Cambridge, Polity.
David, Lennard J. (Ed) (1997) *The Disability Studies Reader*, London, Routledge.
Hales G. 1996 (Ed) *Beyond Disability: Towards an Enabling Society*, London, Sage.
Johnstone, D. (2001) *An Introduction to Disability Studies*, second edition, London, David Fulton Publishers.

Relevant websites of interest

The following are the URLS of only a handful of websites that are of particular interest, but these link to many others as well.

British Council of Disabled People: http://www.bcodp.org.uk/
Centre for Disability Studies: http://www.leeds.ac.uk/disability-studies
Disability Awareness in Action:
 http://www.ourworld.compuserve.com/homepage.DAA_ORG
Disability Net: www.disabilitynet.co.uk
Disability Rights and the law: www.disability.gov.uk/
Evelyn Glennie: www.evelyn.co.uk
Inclusive Education: www.inclusion.uwe.ac.uk
Independent Living: www.independentliving.org/forums/forumframe/html
New Deal for Disabled People: www.dfee/gov.uk/nddp
The Disability Archive: www.leeds.ac.uk/disability-studies/archiveuk/
Tom Shakespeare: www.windmills.u-net.com

22) What's Wrong with "What's Wrong with Libertarianism": a reply to Jeffrey Friedman

(A version of this article first appeared in *Liberty*, vol. 17, no. 8, August 2003.)

Abstract

This essay explains Jeffrey Friedman's two fundamental and persistent philosophical errors concerning the libertarian conception of liberty and the lack of a 'justification' of libertarianism. It is ironic that Friedman himself is thereby revealed to be guilty of both an "a priori" anti-libertarianism and an anti-libertarian "straddle." Critical-rationalist, proactive-imposition-minimising libertarianism remains completely unchallenged by him.

Prefatory note

Some years ago I was a reader and then subscriber of *Critical Review*. I read several of Jeffrey Friedman's series of articles critical of libertarianism in that periodical (of which he was the editor). I noticed that Friedman made two key philosophical errors repeatedly concerning the libertarian conception of liberty and the lack of justification of libertarianism. Eventually, I submitted a response explaining my criticisms. I was told (I paraphrase his letter from memory) that the periodical would now be moving away from philosophy and into public policy, and so if only for this reason he would not be publishing my submission. As I suspected that his own philosophical errors would continue unabated, I found this unsatisfactory. I had it in mind to reply somewhere or other eventually.

Friedman's later article, discussed below, summarises his objections to libertarianism and in the process repeats the errors to which I had objected. Hence it seemed a suitable target for a short restatement of my criticisms (as these were quite different from those of two other replies the article had received, and as Jeffrey Friedman still seems not to have changed his mind since then). Unfortunately, the article below appeared in *Liberty* with an additional introductory paragraph criticising Jeffrey Friedman and *Critical Review* that I had not written, agreed to, or even seen. To be fair, the approaching monthly deadline and computer crashes might have been part of the problem. However, I wish to record that only the text below was submitted or fully sanctioned by me.

Introduction

Jeffrey Friedman's editorship of *Critical Review* has allowed him, publishing in that same periodical, to become one of the most prolific critics of contemporary libertarianism. Many people that take a scholarly interest in libertarianism undoubtedly read him, and presumably he persuades some of them to his anti-libertarian views. He is certainly worth answering. Though others have replied to him before, I think I have a sufficiently different response to make it worth adding my own. I shall reply to one article that encapsulates his main criticisms.

In "What's wrong with libertarianism" (*Critical Review*, 11(3): pp. 407-67), Friedman criticizes libertarianism—as he understands it—usefully focusing on two key points: that libertarianism is empirically unjustified and really held for, inadequate, "philosophical" (*a priori*) reasons; and that libertarians cite empirical evidence in favor of libertarianism but ultimately fall back on the *a priori* reasons. Friedman calls the attempt to be both *a priori* and empirical the "libertarian straddle"

I should say immediately that I believe some of Friedman's criticisms correctly identify errors in certain versions of libertarianism: these versions are overly *a priori* or they are question-begging as regards the conception of liberty. However, his other criticisms are mistaken: they are justificationist (demanding an impossible epistemological support) or misunderstand the libertarian conception of liberty. Ironically, these show Friedman to be guilty of *a priori* anti-libertarianism. And he is also guilty of an anti-libertarian straddle whereby he wants to cite evidence against libertarianism but can always fall back on its lack of justification and its supposed conceptual unclarity. Thus I contend that the most extreme version of non-justificationist libertarianism, as minimizing proactive impositions, remains an unscathed conjecture.

I shall tackle various points in Jeffrey Friedman's "What's wrong with libertarianism" in the order in which they arise. Though Friedman's article is quite lengthy, at almost 25,000 words, I can usefully reply in far less. This is partly because I agree with his oft-restated criticisms of aprioristic libertarianism and the inadequacy of some accounts of libertarian liberty, so I do not need to defend them. And it is partly because his oft-restated justificationist criticisms and his errors about the correct interpretation of libertarian liberty (as opposed to various non-libertarian conceptions of liberty) can best be responded to relatively briefly, as I have a written at length about similar issues in *Escape from Leviathan*.[1]

Friedman's arguments and Lester's responses

Friedman begins his abstract with the assertion that "Libertarian arguments about the empirical benefits of capitalism are, as yet, inadequate to convince anyone who lacks libertarian philosophical convictions" (p. 407). This assertion is itself empirically false. Many British libertarians, including me, were converted—sometimes from socialist ideologies—by "arguments about the empirical benefits". Even if there are no similar American libertarians, which I doubt, I am led to believe that Friedman knows some of the British ones. However, there are always larger-than-normal conjectural leaps in a change of ideology that a justificationist, such as Friedman, might misconstrue as being due to "libertarian philosophical convictions". When Friedman writes of "philosophical libertarianism" he means only an aprioristic version that does not require empirical input. In reality, much or even most libertarian philosophy is intended to complement empirical work. It might be less confusing if Friedman had written of aprioristic libertarianism.

After examining the arguments in several libertarian books, Friedman concludes that "libertarians do not yet possess an adequate critique of government interference in the market economy—a critique, that is to say, that establishes not only why the state should be kept on a very short leash, but why it should be emasculated" (p. 408). The use of "establishes" betrays Friedman's justificationist epistemology. As Karl Popper's critical rationalist epistemology explains, it is illogical to suppose that universal theories can be established with finite evidence (even if such evidence were not itself conjectural, which it is). But that does not mean that we cannot validly advance bold universal conjectures that we test as best we can. However, Friedman combines his epistemological error with other philosophical ones that reinforce it, as we shall see.

Friedman thinks that a "purely consequentialist, 'empirical' libertarianism could, on its own, largely accept as valid the meliorist aims listed by Cornuelle, challenging mainly whether the state is capable of achieving them without causing even worse problems" (p. 409). But when libertarians have read of research and economic theory that appear to refute all the assertions that the state is the solution, rather than the problem, it is hard to see how they could see any list of "meliorist aims" as being other than due largely to empirical misunderstandings. It would be equally presumptuous for libertarians to assert that purely consequentialist, 'empirical' anti-libertarianism could, on its own, largely accept as valid the meliorist aims of libertarianism, challenging mainly whether the market is capable of achieving them without causing even worse problems.

Justificationism arises again in the statement that "[l]ibertarian conclusions require not only extensive evidence of government failure, but an empirically substantiated reason to think that such failure is always more likely than the failure of civil society" (p. 410). An "empirically substantiated reason"—especially that something is "*always* more likely"—is not an epistemological possibility. But a critical preference for a conjecture is possible. In order to maintain a critical preference for the libertarian conjecture one need only refute putative examples of government success. Friedman's main criticism of the market—for he focuses only on this aspect of libertarianism—is that there is no guarantee that it is and will "always" be better than state intervention. As this is an impossible demand (and one to which John Gray also succumbs, as I explain in *Escape from Leviathan*), this criticism amounts, ironically, to a kind of philosophical anti-libertarianism (more precisely, aprioristic anti-libertarianism). This is every bit as erroneous as the so-called philosophical libertarianism that Friedman is attacking.

But now consider the other main issue, from my perspective, that Friedman raises. Does the state deprive people of freedom (or liberty)? Friedman thinks that it does not because he misunderstands the libertarian conception of interpersonal liberty, as do many libertarians themselves, as involving the absence of "coercion" in some sense. And as all property systems use coercion to enforce themselves, he is able to conclude that "strictly in terms of negative liberty—freedom from physical coercion—libertarianism has no edge over any other system" (p. 428). However, an analysis of the *libertarian* conception of interpersonal liberty shows it to be about what I formulate as 'the absence of proactive impositions' (though I am not claiming that this formula is perspicuously clear and without philosophical problems). And all property assignments, including that of self-ownership, are derivable from applying this conception. It is true that interfering with the (libertarian) property of others will count as a proactive imposition as a very good rule of thumb. But the abstract theory need not assume any kind of property, nor moral rights. Thus Friedman errs in concluding that "Boaz is mistaken in describing taxation as 'aggression against the person or property of the taxpayer'." Because the "social-democratic baseline" is inherently proactive in its impositions and so does flout libertarian liberty. I cannot usefully summarize all the relevant arguments here. Any attempt to do so would merely give rise to the myriad further questions and criticisms that I discuss in *Escape from Leviathan*. However, once one grasps that libertarian liberty is about the absence of proactive impositions (or some similar formulation) one can easily understand the general dangers of infringing such liberty and why the onus of argument must be on those who advocate doing so.

I claim that my interpretation of the libertarian conception of liberty is what libertarians intuitively grasp, though they do not express it clearly. But having mistakenly discussed a Hobbesian, zero-sum, freedom instead, Friedman decides that it is better to choose "positive freedom", which is the ability to "attain a goal" we choose (p. 431). As this is clearly about want-satisfaction, I see it as about a kind of welfare rather than any kind of liberty (though it does not much matter what terms we use). Friedman then suggests that "the social democrat wants to equalize positive freedom, but more rigorously than does the libertarian." The libertarian does not want any such thing. He wants to maximize interpersonal liberty (minimize proactive impositions). He might well think, as I do, that this will also maximize want-satisfaction. But to "equalize" the ability to "attain a goal" we choose is nothing to do with libertarianism. Friedman's view that libertarians "would arbitrarily extend positive liberty only to those who happen to have acquired title to pieces of the world" is confused just because libertarians typically suppose that (libertarian) private property clashes less with getting more of what you want than any known alternative. And Friedman, as usual, offers little argument or evidence to the contrary beyond mere logical possibility.

None of what I have written entails that the libertarian conception of liberty is intended to be the "correct" conception of liberty or its "essence", as Friedman accuses libertarians of intending (p. 431). But there is something that *libertarian* liberty is and it is not what Friedman supposes nor is it advocated for the reasons he supposes. So Friedman is mistaken in his assertion that "[t]he assumption that liberty is embodied in libertarianism relatively more than in other systems is necessarily false, however—unless we are speaking of positive liberty..." (p. 433). For liberty as the absence of proactive impositions (or some similar formulation)—which Friedman fails to begin to suspect—is necessarily more embodied in libertarianism.

So with my preferred version of libertarianism I can accurately invert Friedman's charge, thus: "The way [anti-]libertarianism incorporates consequentialist and philosophical arguments feeds on and breeds complacency at the same time" (p. 433). Instead of complaining that "consequentialist libertarians do not yet appear to have established a valid reason why government intervention in a free-market economy might not sometimes be better at meeting human needs than laissez faire", when such a reason is logically impossible, why does Friedman not attempt to give, what *is* logically possible, one real example of government success (p. 438)? He surely does attempt to do this on other occasions, and he mentions public goods and the need for economic redistribution in his article. But when he does so he always has his philosophical anti-libertarianism to fall back on: libertarians cannot justify the thesis that they must always be right. So we can again invert his accusation, thus: "Divine intervention might seem to be the only thing that could make sense of this [anti-]libertarian straddle: the notion that one need not choose between *a priori* and *a posteriori* rationales for a[n anti-]libertarian world (although, if one had to choose, one would choose the *a priori* rationale) ..." (p. 435).

Consistent with his justificationist approach, Friedman writes that occasionally "Boaz does make consequentialist arguments of sufficient generality to justify libertarianism, if they are sound" (p. 439). Obviously Friedman must think they are unsound. Justificationists typically have higher standards of 'justification' for things they do not currently accept. Friedman doubtless thinks that diZerega is 'justified' in his view that "democracy is a spontaneous order" (p. 439). But as he does not give any argument to this effect I merely note that democracy is proactively imposed, and hence cannot be spontaneous. And presumably Friedman also feels fully justified in asserting that "there remain, at the very least, some public goods and, in principle, the need for economic redistribution" (p. 445). Which public goods? Why is there a need, in principle, for economic redistribution? We are not told, so cannot reply. It is enough for Friedman that he knows these things to be justified.

It might be generally true, I do not know, that "[a]mong libertarian economists there is a parallel conviction that a sound philosophical case for libertarianism has already been made—by libertarian philosophers" (p. 448). However, this is certainly not true of all libertarian economists or of David Friedman in particular. David Friedman tends to scorn libertarian philosophy—I answer his criticisms from *The Machinery of Freedom* in *Escape from Leviathan*—and presents only consequentialist arguments. Why does Jeffrey Friedman ignore this prominent example? We then return to the justificationist error with Friedman's assertion that "[a]ll of the painstaking research of Chicago- and Austrian-school economists could not explain why every government regulation, let alone every government redistribution of wealth, would necessarily do more harm than good" (p. 450). So what? How can Friedman seriously complain about the absence of logically *necessary* proofs of the superiority of *every* possible libertarian policy?

Near the end of his article Friedman suggests that libertarians are "precluded by their own ideology—which effectively celebrates whatever consumers freely choose as, *ipso facto*, good—from criticizing consumerism" (p. 453). Nobody is trapped in an ideology, though it might prompt him to a certain position at the start of an argument. It would be as idle to say that Friedman is precluded by his own anti-libertarian ideology from understanding certain things. Of course Friedman is, in a sense, "precluded" by his philosophical and empirical views from accepting libertarianism. But he is not precluded from coming to understand that these are errors, if they are so.

Friedman has done a good service in emphasizing the inadequacy of a certain libertarian philosophical position. However, because of inadequacies in his own "philosophical" anti-libertarianism and his anti-libertarian straddle, nothing he has written in "What's Wrong With Libertarianism" is a threat to libertarianism properly understood. Friedman has presented no argument and cited no evidence that criticizes critical-rationalist (or non-justificationist) libertarianism (as minimizing proactive impositions). Justificationist anti-libertarianism is a futile endeavour. But I do not doubt that Friedman can, and I certainly hope that he will, move on to non-justificationist anti-libertarianism.

Note

[1] Lester, J. C. [2000] 2012. *Escape from Leviathan: Libertarianism Without Justificationism*. Buckingham: The University of Buckingham Press.

23) A Sceptical Look at "A Skeptical Look at Karl Popper"[1]

(Libertarian Alliance online, 2004.)

Prefatory note

This article is about critical rationalism and hence not about libertarianism directly. However, epistemologically, I advocate critical-rationalist libertarianism. And there have already been several references to Popper, critical rationalism, and the impossibility of epistemological justifications—not least in the previous reply to Jeffrey Friedman. Hence it would seem to be an omission not to include something more explicit and detailed on the matter. The following reply to Martin Gardner seems to fulfil the role adequately here.

> "Martin Gardner / Required an intellectual-sin pardoner / As a 'skeptic' who fell for induction / Despite hypothetico-deductive instruction." A clerihew by Juan Hoo Gnoes

It is an irony to attack a more sceptical epistemology than one's own in the name of scepticism and defend, instead, an epistemology that is positively illogical. And yet that is what Martin Gardner has done in his "A Skeptical Look at Karl Popper." In this reply I shall give my own responses, which might differ somewhat from those of other "Popperians" (I am happy to be called a critical rationalist, but I doubt many admirers of Popper subscribe to every Popperian theory). If I repeat similar points in places that is because Gardner repeats the same errors, and I do not want to let any of them by as though they might be acceptable. But I shall ignore Gardner's attacks on Popper's character as mere *ad hominem* slurs.

Gardner tells us that Popper's "followers among philosophers of science are a diminishing minority, convinced that Popper's vast reputation is enormously inflated". If Popper's "followers among philosophers of science are a diminishing minority" then so much the worse for the philosophy of science. But such a sociological statistic is irrelevant to the truth of Popper's theories. If it is supposed to be a reason to ignore Popper's actual arguments, as Gardner does, then it combines the fallacies of arguing from authority (a decidedly tarnished authority) and arguing from what the majority believe. It is surely not true that

Popper's "followers ... are ... convinced that Popper's vast reputation is enormously inflated."

Is it true that "Popper's reputation was based mainly on [his] persistent but misguided efforts to restate common-sense views in a novel language"? To take two examples, how can Popper's Quasi-Platonic World Three or his view that scientific theories are completely without evidential support be "common-sense views in a novel language"? Gardner wants especially to criticise the second example, Popper's epistemology. He writes that Popper argues that confirmation "is slow and never certain". It is not slow. It does not start. How can finite instances begin to confirm a universal theory? So "all crows are black" does not entail that "[e]very find of another black crow obviously confirms the theory."

It is a muddle (throughout Gardner's article) to conflate Popper's general argument about universal cases, which cannot be observed, with particular instances, which can. We cannot see all crows being black but we might see a particular crow being black (though even this remains theory-laden). Thus "water on Mars" is not an example of Popper's view of a universal scientific theory. But in any case, neither, strictly speaking, can there be "confirming instances" of "water on Mars." Rather, there are only theory-laden interpretations of apparent evidence that pass the available tests. It is entirely irrelevant to the epistemological arguments whether or not astronomers themselves "do not think they are making efforts to falsify the conjecture."

We are told that "Falsifications can be as fuzzy and elusive as confirmations." That falsifications can be difficult in practice does not affect the simple logic of a single assumed instance refuting a universal theory. By contrast, confirmations are not possible just because even particular examples of a crow's being black have an indefinitely large number of implicit universal aspects (such as, it is always a black crow even when no one is observing it), some being counterfactual (such as, it would die if deprived of oxygen for one hour). I take 'confirmation' to be an inductivist term, at least as Gardner intends it, implying support. Thus even a basic statement is not confirmed or supported. It too is a conjecture. People might think they are looking for confirmations, but epistemologically they can only ever find corroborations—in Popper's intended sense of compatible, but not supporting, theory-laden evidence (if they are not typographical or scanning errors, I assume Gardner slips when he uses "conformation" and "conforming" a couple of times: a conformation sounds more like a corroboration).

Observations of black crows, it is stated, "can be taken in two ways; confirmations of 'all crows are black,' or disconfirmations of 'some crows are not black.'" How can a single observation of a black crow (even if accurate) support a universal theory? How can it undermine the existential statement that there is a non-black crow somewhere? Gardner makes his assertions without attempting to reply to these obvious falsificationist criticisms. It is true that "Popper recognized—but dismissed as unimportant—that every falsification of a conjecture is simultaneously a confirmation of an opposite conjecture." 'All crows are black' has the form of a universal theory in science. The assumption 'This is a white crow' falsifies it and is significant. The fact that 'This is a white crow' also logically confirms the theory 'Not all crows are black' (assuming this is the "opposite conjecture") is without scientific significance. 'Not all crows are black' does not have the form of a universal theory in science. Gardner continues, "and every conforming [sic] instance of a conjecture is a falsification of an opposite conjecture." To make sense of this I can only assume that the "opposite conjecture" to 'All crows are black' is now 'No crows are black' (or some equivalent expression). But that is a universal conjecture that "This is a black crow" significantly falsifies.

Gardner supposes that the following is an example of how confirmation and falsification are linked in practice: "If a giant atom smasher ... detects a Higgs, it will confirm the conjecture that the field exist[s]. At the same time it will falsify ... that there *is* no Higgs field." There are various confusions here. The detection of an apparent single Higgs particle is not the detection of a universal field. That would be like saying that the detection of an apparent black crow is the detection of universal black crowness (all crows being black). So the apparent detection of a Higgs particle cannot confirm the universal theory (and it is a highly theory-laden singular, in any case). It can only corroborate it. If we assume that it is a single Higgs particle (because it might be and we cannot fault the experiment or think of an alternative theory to explain the particle), then that assumption logically falsifies only 'there are no Higgs particles'. But the assumption is not epistemologically confirmed. Of course, we might also grant the assumption that there is a Higgs field (because there might be and we cannot fault the experiment or think of an alternative theory to explain *this type* of particle). Obviously, that assumption would logically falsify the conjecture "there *is* no Higgs field". But, *a fortiori*, that universal assumption is not epistemologically confirmed.

So we have no sound argument from Gardner that "science operates mainly by induction (confirmation), and also and less often by disconfirmation (falsification)." And although there are logical and conceptual links between them, induction (inferring from particular instances to some general thesis) is not the same as epistemological confirmation (that single instances make a general theory more probable). Further, it is again entirely epistemologically irrelevant that with scientists and philosophers in the 'inductive fold' (to invert Gardner's gibe), "[i]ts language is almost always one of induction." What is the relevance of Gardner's joke that "If Popper bet on a certain horse to win a race, and the horse won, you would not expect him to shout, 'Great! My horse failed to lose!'" Gardner thinks that Popper ought to shout this if he were consistent about denying confirmations. But Popper's point is, again, that we can observe (albeit in a theory-laden way) such singular events as a horse winning but we cannot observe universals, such as 'My horse always wins' (even if it has done so in all observed cases).

In what way is discovering that "smaller and smaller planets orbit distant suns" supposed to be "inductive evidence that there may be Earth-sized planets out there"? Gardner simply asserts the existence of induction without explaining how the inference could possibly work. However, 'There are no other Earth-sized planets' *is* a universal conjecture that the discovery of one would falsify. But the apparent discovery of one will be a singular (though theory-laden and not confirmed) observation and not itself a universal scientific theory. (But why should there not be other Earth-sized planets if no theory makes the Earth special? The absence of such a theory is what mainly makes plausible the conjecture that they exist.) So astronomers can obtain only a (conjectural) falsification of the universal theory, even if it is true that they consider themselves to be "inductivists who seek positive conformations [sic]". It is absurd of Gardner to appeal to scientists' opinions to solve an epistemological problem. It is like appealing to their opinions on whether genetic engineering is moral.

How, exactly, do prediction and explanation relate to "classical induction procedures"? Without an explanation Gardner may as well assert they are part of classical magic procedures. It leaves us with nothing substantial to criticise. The quotation from Nagel that Popper's falsificationism "is close to being a caricature of scientific procedures" again reveals the confusion of sociology with epistemology.

I cannot understand why Gardner thinks that 'corroboration' is just 'confirmation' but, supposedly like Popper's other terms, "restated ... in a bizarre and cumbersome terminology." The assertion that the apparent evidence merely *fits* (corroborates) some universal theory, which is possible, is clearly quite different from the assertion that the evidence positively *supports* (confirms) some universal theory, which is impossible. Is there no difference between asserting something that is possible and asserting something that is impossible? And to be impressed by the fact that a theory made novel predictions and was not falsified is not to be covertly inductivist. True theories will pass all the tests we can come up with, provided that the tests are carried out correctly. And true theories are what we seek.

Popper did not, as others had done, "point out that science, unlike math and logic, is never absolutely certain." He pointed out that science is absolutely uncertain. Quite a different proposition (consider the difference between being 'not absolutely bullet proof' and being 'absolutely not bullet proof'). And mathematics and logic are not that certain either. This is a far more extreme form of scepticism than that of most who accept "fallibilism". However, it is compatible with this view that we can attain truth nevertheless: as truth is a metaphysical correspondence between a theory and the world it describes. Either a theory or its negation is true. So we have a 50% chance of success merely by a random selection of the two.

Popper's *propensity* theory of probability applies to single instances and flouts determinism. As I understand it, the standard frequency theory does not apply to single instances and is compatible with determinism. Mathematicians undoubtedly use probability in a way that fits well with the propensity interpretation, but they leave it undefined. So, again, how is this, "introducing a new term which says nothing different from what can be better said in conventional terminology"?

In my view, in *The Open Society and Its Enemies* Popper's refutation of Marx is relatively flimsy[2] and his defence of liberal democracy is significantly at odds with his epistemology and methodology.[3] Yet Gardner praises it as his "most impressive work" with "powerful arguments and awesome erudition" (though I concede that it does contain these as well despite the two crucial aforementioned flaws).

Gardner concludes his criticisms by saying that "[c]onfirming instances underlie our beliefs that the Sun will rise tomorrow, that dropped objects will fall, that water will freeze and boil, and a million other events. It is hard to think of another philosophical battle so decisively lost." But since these theories were first formulated we have discovered that the sun does not always 'rise' each day in the North and South poles (and does not really 'rise', at all), that a 'dropped' hot air balloon will not fall, that water will not freeze or boil at normal temperatures given unusual pressures, and a million other refutations of things we thought we once knew. In any case, Gardner is again implicitly confusing sociology with epistemology. And it is even too early to give a sociological appraisal. Today's counterintuitive theory can become tomorrow's common sense. Perhaps the modern equivalent of Descartes's deceiving demon is that we live in a Matrix-like virtual reality (though this has obvious parallels with Berkeley's view of the world as well). As ordinary cinema-goers do not seem to have any problem with understanding that this is at least a logical possibility, then they presumably see that apparent 'confirming instances' of everyday life must count for nothing as an argument against it. (But this is not to suggest that it is true or that there cannot be cogent philosophical arguments that it is false.)

Finally, as he thinks it "one of the best" books by a "Popperian", it is a pity that Gardner did not attempt to reply to any of the actual arguments in *Critical Rationalism: A Restatement and Defence* (1994), by David Miller (the unnamed "top acolyte"). Consider, for instance, the claim made in Chapter 3 that if you 'confirm' a hypothesis you learn nothing (because you had already predicted that result) but if you refute it you learn something. But then Gardner has not dealt seriously with any of Popper's arguments either. It is much to be regretted that Gardner, who years ago published an excellent book critically dissecting *Fads and Fallacies in the Name of Science*, has now reached the stage of uncritically genuflecting to fads and fallacies in philosophy.

Notes

[1] Martin Gardner, "A Skeptical Look at Karl Popper," *Skeptical Inquirer*, 2001, 25(4):13-14, 72.
[2] For a more robust refutation see David Ramsay Steele, *From Marx to Mises: Post-capitalist Society and the Challenge of Economic Calculation*, Open Court, 1992.
[3] J C Lester, *Escape from Leviathan: Liberty, Welfare and Anarchy Reconciled*, Macmillan/St Martin's Press, 2000, 135-142.

24) Statement on the London Bombings

(Libertarian Alliance online, 2005.)

Islamic bombers have finally hit London. Why has this happened and what can be done to stop it?

Bombings by Islamic terrorists against the West have occurred only in countries, or against human targets, where their governments have attacked and intervened in Muslim states or lands with a majority Muslim population. September the 11th occurred after many years of US-state interventions and bombings around the world (including the military action against Iraq in 1991), and vast financial and military support for Israel, including its actions against predominantly Muslim Palestinians and other Muslim countries.

In retaliation for the deaths of September 11th, even more innocent civilians in Afghanistan were bombed to death by the Bush-Blair axis, and the country was then occupied while civilian deaths continue to this day. If they had wanted to catch Osama bin Laden without being cowardly mass murderers, then they should instead have landed troops directly and immediately on the mountains where he was suspected of hiding.

By the best available estimate, during the 2003 invasion of Iraq around 100,000 innocent civilians died, many murdered directly by the Bush-Blair axis bombings, and the country was then occupied while civilian deaths continue to this day.[1] If they had wanted to deal with Saddam Hussein without being cowardly mass murderers, then they should, again, have targeted him directly or put a price on his head.

The Bush-Blair axis is the leading world terrorist organisation against foreign Muslims. As even many ordinary people now see and state, finally echoing long-held government security services warnings, in this way Bush and Blair have inevitably made our countries targets for terrorist retaliation.

There is never any excuse for bombing innocent people. The terrorists in London have sunk to the level of Bush and Blair. They might, instead, have done what Bush and Blair failed to do and directly targeted the guilty men: Bush and Blair themselves. Then they would not be terrorists, but vigilantes.

What should the UK-state do now? Two things: withdraw all troops from around the world; and put Anthony Charles Lynton Blair, and his fellow conspirators, on trial for war crimes. Withdrawing all troops is an immediate practical possibility. Unfortunately, Blair's trial is not yet likely. But withdrawing all troops would considerably diminish, if not entirely stop, the terrorism.

Note

[1] Les Roberts, Riyadh Lafta, Richard Garfield, Jamal Khudhairi, and Gilbert Burnham, "Mortality before and after the 2003 Invasion of Iraq: Cluster Sample Survey", *The Lancet*, vol. 364 (2004):1857-64.

25) Nozick's Flawless Libertarianism? A Book Review

(On *On Nozick*, by Edward Feser. Libertarian Alliance online, 2004.)

This is an excellent though largely uncritical introduction to, and defence of, Robert Nozick's *Anarchy, State and Utopia* (New York: Basic Books, 1974). It is also quite a good introduction to libertarianism. It is full of good arguments. I shall confine myself to critical remarks. My responses are mainly in the order that matters arise in the book.

First, three brief linguistic points. Which proof reader of Wadsworth's allowed "30's", etc., (p. 11 and throughout) without striking out the otiose apostrophe? As an anarchist, I should rather say that liberty ought to be the highest *social* value (or rule) rather than "political value" (p. 11). Feser apparently uses, as do many libertarians, the English word 'coercion' to mean not coercion (the use, or threat, of force to constrain or compel some person—possibly in libertarian self-defence or rectification) but to mean any liberty/rights violation even where no coercion is involved (p. 14). He does not do this persistently, though.

In explaining the "impossibility of socialism" Feser does not mention that this is usually known as the economic calculation argument (p. 18). Neither does he quite spell out what the problem is: that the planners have no way of determining the *relative* scarcity of resources. Then, having apparently argued for the "impossibility of socialism", Feser writes of "the socialist economies of the communist world" finally collapsing in the 1980s: "Mises and Hayek predicted, as far back as the 1920's, that this is exactly what would happen" (p. 20). This is a confusion. Mises argued that Marxian socialism is, as Feser earlier noted, *impossible*. There is no known substitute for the price system to determine relative scarcity in an advanced industrial society. Socialism did not collapse after many decades, it was a non-starter. The USSR had a price system, albeit even more state-interfered-with than our own, and thus was not socialist in the sense that Mises was criticising. Of course, there are other senses of 'socialism' and Mises's argument when generalised applies to them as being inefficient *to the extent that* they override the price system. But they are not what Mises's argument was primarily about. And though Mises's book on socialism was published in 1922, the Hayek-edited *Collectivist Economic Planning: Critical Studies on the Possibilities of Socialism* did not appear until 1935.

Feser objects that "Classical utilitarianism ... leaves open the possibility that some people may be appropriately sacrificed ..." (p. 32).

This is a logical possibility, but is it a real one? Correctly interpreted, I do not think so. A utilitarian might equally well reply that 'libertarian rights leave open the possibility that some people may be left to starve.' That does not seem to be very likely either. And if observing rights is supposed to accord with "respect for human dignity" then so can promoting human welfare. The practical point is that there does not seem to be a real clash between the two. Defenders of rights through most of history would think it strange to attempt to divorce human rights from human welfare and then take sides.

We are told that "unless we assume the thesis of self-ownership, we have no way of explaining *why* certain things are wrong that clearly are wrong. The thesis of self-ownership is, then, as plausible and fundamental a moral principle as there could be" (p. 33). It is not much of an 'explanation' to insist that the explanation has to stop at the assumption of self-ownership. We can go on to explain how not allowing self-ownership leads to disastrous "moral hazards" (mentioned by Feser [p. 35]) for both liberty (more abstractly defined than just being self-ownership, of course[1]) and welfare. We might even concede that in special extreme cases where self-ownership can harm either liberty or welfare, the case for absolute self-ownership might be morally weakened.[2] Thus we can derive general self-ownership from both liberty[3] and welfare.[4] So self-ownership is not itself "as plausible and fundamental a moral principle as there could be."

It sounds quasi-Marxist and slightly misleading to say that if self-ownership is true "I also own the *products* of my abilities, talents, and labor, that is, whatever wealth I produce in using them" (p. 34). For if I produce something for you under contract, then I need not at any point own the thing I physically produce or all the wealth it brings. And though I own the money that you pay me for the contractual work, I did not really produce that money and neither did you (unless, perhaps, at least one of us literally produces notes or coins).

Is it true that the "negative" nature of rights means that there is no "danger that they might conflict" (p. 38)? To take only one classic example, what if person A buys all the land surrounding person B and then refuses to allow B to leave B's land? Does A have an 'inviolable' right to refuse to allow B to cross his property? Or does B have an 'inviolable' right not to be arbitrarily imprisoned? It is such examples that, to my mind, require a libertarian theory of liberty that is anterior to, and more abstract than, both self-ownership and ownership of external property.

I do not know what it means to assert that persons are "free by nature" (p. 39). I certainly think that people ought to be free, in the libertarian sense, and that they are better off being so. I also think this moral principle withstands critical scrutiny. But why are people free "by nature"? Is this supposed to be a moral law that is discovered in nature like a natural law such as gravity? Feser later glosses "natural" as "not derived from or dependent on any human agreements or conventions" (p. 43). But in what way does that make human freedom part of 'nature'? I know 'natural law' has a long history, but more needs to be said to make sense of, and defend, it than the few words Feser expends.

Does libertarianism need foundations? Feser considers various possibilities in addition to self-ownership (pp. 48-53). For the critical rationalist, however, the idea that respecting individual liberty is morally desirable remains a conjecture. It is sufficient that there is no known sound reason to interfere with individual liberty (in any systematic or institutional way, at least). Any search for positively justifying this view runs into the epistemological problem that we never know what refuting counter-instance or counter-argument we might have overlooked (or even which corroborating examples might convince some people). There is also the problem of an infinite regress if we try to support libertarianism by a more fundamental principle such as enabling humans to pursue 'virtue,' or 'flourish,' or be 'project pursuers,' or have 'autonomy.' In any case, surely libertarians allow that people have the right to be vicious (if at no one else's imposed expense), to 'wither,' to do nothing much, or be heteronomous.

Feser also mentions the idea that the very use of one's body presupposes self-ownership and so one cannot argue against it "without falling into a pragmatic self-contradiction" (p. 50). It seems to be true that in using one's body one presupposes that one has a right to do so, but only if (as I accept, following Socrates and contradicting Aristotle) it is not possible to do what one genuinely believes to be wrong at the time. But it is not a logical inference that one does have the right just because one must presuppose it in a live argument. If there were an omnipotent god and he (decided that he) owned us, then he would own us whatever our arguments on the matter.

In the end, Feser concludes that the burden of proof lies with the critics, "It is not *Nozick* who needs to 'provide foundations' for or justify his libertarianism, then—it is his *critics* who need to justify themselves" (p. 54). And the typical welfare statist no doubt shares an equal and opposite view. So we would appear to have a stalemate of each side demanding justification from the other. But no one can provide foundations for their conjectures. When they think they are doing so they are at best explaining how they think their theory will usually apply. It is better to seek, and provide, and address criticism.

Feser sees that protection agencies will "settle disputes between clients by appealing to a neutral third party" (p. 58). But he appears to think that it must be the *same* "third party ... which numerous firms retain" for all disputes. This is an error: the fallacy of composition. It is sufficient that all protection agencies have bilateral contracts for settling disputes (possibly by some default procedure in the absence of a specifically named third agency; maybe even selecting one by lottery). There is no need for a single agency to arise as the one to which all must ultimately appeal. And any two agencies can change their chosen third party at any time they agree to do so. Thus there is no tendency "toward a kind of natural monopoly ... a single dominant agency or a single confederation of agencies ...." And so there is no need for "common arbitration procedures." There can be healthy competition among procedures. Some people might still think that there is a sort of overall 'monopoly system' here. But it is no more a monopoly than exists among banks just because *all* banks have bilateral agreements on how to deal with each other concerning charges, accepting cheques, etc. Therefore, there is no reason for a minimal state to emerge by overruling competing agencies that are outside the 'monopoly.'

It is not a "loss of one's full *liberty*" (contra Feser) to become dependent on the state (p. 73). It is, rather, the gain of a licence. It is only a loss of liberty to be forced to pay for this dependence by others.

Nozick argues, and Feser agrees, that taxation is "on a par with forced labor" (p. 77ff). Immoral and inefficient though taxation is, it is not on a par with forced labour. It is 'only' extortion (and only for those who really pay it; not those who are net tax-consumers, possibly by working for the state). It cannot be on a par with forced labour for the simple reason that no one is forced to labour. If you sit about doing no work then no one will make you work. Quite the reverse, you will in effect be paid by the welfare state for not working. If you do work—in the private sector, at least—then extortion by the state is difficult to avoid (but you should do your best). Anyway, it would be possible to abolish income tax and replace it with sales tax. Then the retailers alone would be forced to hand over money to the state, and not for working as such (though some work is thereby made necessary). Still less is the so-called welfare state, terrible though it is, a system of "*partial* slavery" (p. 79). There are countries that really do have forced labour and partial slavery. The victims there would rightly see that they are not on a par with those who merely pay income tax. The answer to Nozick's "Tale of a Slave" question (p. 80) is that this is a form of the sorites problem (how many grains of sand make a pile?). Your situation becomes less and less slave-like until it is clearly hyperbole to assert that you are a slave. Otherwise, at a still farther extreme, you would still be a 'slave' if only the mildest imposition were to (threaten to) occur only once in your life. You remain, however, a *subject*—even if you think you are a 'free citizen'—of aggressively imposed state rule. And that is bad enough.

Feser tries to muddle through with Nozick's defence of the Lockean labour-mixing (or what-you-own-mixing) theory of initial acquisition. Feser thinks it is "*significantly* to alter a resource or bring it under one's control that effectively turns it into property" (p. 83). Why can I not simply use or rely on some resource (such as a natural water hole, which example Feser later mentions) without significantly altering it or controlling it? What if I significantly alter and control a resource (maybe by damming a small stream in sport) but do not care a jot about it? How *exactly* does significant alteration or control relate to *liberty*? What is the explicit connection? We seem to have, rather, an appeal to a pre-existing vague intuition. If (interpersonal) liberty is more precisely conceived as not being proactively imposed on by other people (to take an example not entirely at random), then it is sufficient that I merely rely on the water hole for me to have some libertarian property claims not to be excluded by someone fencing it off—especially if it is the only water around. Feser later concedes a property claim here (p. 87) but does not square it with the labour-mixing that involves significant alteration or control. If it is true that reliance can be enough, then it is not true that 'labor-mixing of some sort seems the only available way of getting property started' (p. 83). And labour-mixed property can sometimes clash with liberty.

He goes further, however, and denies that there can be any injustice in *initial* acquisitions because no one has any libertarian rights until acquisition takes place (p. 86). Feser suggests that for A to be the *first* to monopolise a water hole and deny others access would be "callous, cruel and wicked" but not unjust because "it's A's water hole" (p. 87). Why should being there first *always* be trumps as regards *liberty*? A is here being a positive nuisance (or worse, if death by thirst ensues) to other people. He is not protecting the fruits of his labours in any way. So there is no sound analogy between this and merely failing to assist someone by, in Feser's example, not helping him to start his car. The distinction between proactively imposing and merely failing to assist is the crucial abstraction that is required to make sense of the liberty of libertarianism.

In short, I think that Feser does not have adequate arguments to respond to contrary arguments in my own philosophical defence of anarcho-libertarianism as maximising liberty and welfare (despite citing my book in his bibliography). I hope I have not been unfair or unclear in attempting to restate some of my views in response to his defence of Nozick's book. It was largely my perceived inadequacies of *Anarchy, State, and Utopia* that spurred me to write something rather different. But Feser is a bright libertarian who has merely fallen among justificationists, minarchists and Aristotelians.

Notes

[1] J C Lester, *Escape from Leviathan: Liberty, Welfare and Anarchy Reconciled*, Macmillan/St Martin's Press, 2000, 57-61.
[2] Ibid. 65-66.
[3] Ibid. 76
[4] Ibid. 185-187

26) An Attack on the Realm: a Book Review

(On *In Defence of the Realm: The Place of Nations in Classical Liberalism*, by David Conway. Libertarian Alliance online, 2005.)

This book has many arguments doing an excellent job of dismantling the positions of those who would have the state do considerably more than defend the national realm. Thus far, it is hard for me to fault it—which is more difficult when one is already in agreement: the ideologically opposed can often provide more useful criticisms. But, as the book's title indicates, it does not go all the way to anarcho-liberalism (in fact, it does not even fully embody certain basic tenets of classical liberalism). And as its criticisms of anarcho-liberalism—or private-property anarchy—are those to which I am ideologically opposed, I shall mainly concentrate on those.

David Conway objects to the view that "liberal states must open their doors to unlimited immigration, even where the number of immigrants exceeds that which resources can sustain or which is incompatible with the survival of the indigenous culture" (p. 35). Thus we have a version of the overpopulation scare in the first part of this objection to unlimited immigration. And then we have the idea that the indigenous culture cannot survive and, implicitly, that it has a right to do so.

Many involved with population studies, not least Julian Simon (1932-1998),[1] have often pointed out that the entire population of the world could comfortably live in the space of a small country—the size of Yugoslavia, used to be cited by some—with the population density of a modern city—say, New York—throughout (though some resources might then need to be imported, as they are with cities). Thus it is hopelessly mistaken to think that the current UK or the USA lands are 'full' and that more people must simply mean fewer resources for all and lower output per head. On the contrary, the more that come in the more the division of labour will tend to raise the wealth of those in that area (even if we were not to have private streets and were to continue to have wasteful state 'welfare', etc.). In fact, if this Mad Hatter's "No room! No room!" thesis were true, then it would seem that all human reproduction beyond replacement level, at most, ought to be discouraged.

What right has an "indigenous culture" to survive? Such cultures inevitably change over time even within the territories of nation-states. However, if people choose to maintain a certain way of life then there is no reason that it must perish. The Amish in the USA, for instance, can happily continue as long as people wish to practice that way of life; no matter how few their numbers relative to the growing and heterogeneous cultures in the USA. Of course, many might chose to allow their culture to be changed by mixing with their new neighbours in terms of custom or even reproduction. That is their choice and it would illiberal to prevent it. Conway says his real fear, which he elaborates later, is that the new illiberal cultures will crush the existing liberal ones or make the overall state illiberal. But this assumes a state is needed for policing and defence (rather than inevitably growing at the expense of liberalism and security), so we'll come back to this where he puts his arguments for these.

I should add, however, that many dislike the multi-racial society—including many of the people who have, nevertheless, chosen to migrate into such a society (but it is a modern taboo to admit to such popular 'racism' in the mass media). This external cost can best be internalised, albeit imperfectly, by allowing those who wish to do so to live separately by using private property, not least in the streets, to discriminate as regards who associates with them (for the civil liberty known as 'freedom of association' also includes the right *not* to associate with people).

Conway avers that "towards their own state and its public places, citizens stand in a significantly different relation than aliens do. Unlike aliens, citizens can be regarded as co-owners of these 'public places'. ... no sound liberal principle ... [is] contravened by states that grant their own citizens the liberty to leave and re-enter their territories but deny that same liberty to aliens" (p. 39). Note first, that this rejection of the free movement of people ("aliens") across national borders even flouts a standard tenet of classical liberalism. But a libertarian deconstruction of this position makes things clearest. Our state is our "own state" in much the way that a slave's master is his 'own master'. The slave's 'own' master actually owns the slave and the state approaches owning us: the state rules us; we do not rule it, despite very occasionally electing the oligarchy that rules us in the name of democracy. Neither do we state subjects (for a "citizen" in the political sense is still a subject of the state, albeit with some 'rights' the state allows him *pro tem*) own the "public places". Members of the public might be allowed to go there, but the state really owns them and decides on the rules, just like any private-property owner. By contrast, we ought fully to own ourselves and the 'public places' should be fully privately owned outside the state. Then the particular street owners, etc., would be able to decide what rules, and who, to allow in their streets, parks, squares, and so on. For though liberalism is clearly incompatible with restrictions on immigration into a state territory (the 'realm'), it is further required by libertarianism that the various private owners can then decide what suits them. Whatever it chooses, the state imposes on its existing subjects and any excluded would-be immigrants by using aggressive coercion (as it is not defending the persons and property of legitimate property owners) to impose its will.

In his criticisms of libertarianism, Conway first supposes a "state" set up by contract. Who could complain if this state were as effective in offering people protection as "it was reasonable to imagine any private agency could?" (p. 65). And who could complain if he were taxed for this? As I do not believe that concepts have essences, I suppose I should grant the assumption that a 'state' could conceivably be set up by universal contract (however implausible, in reality, that might be). Such a state would be entirely libertarian (with respect to the existing generation of contractors, at least), for those who contracted in would have bound themselves and not been proactively imposed on. In which case, even if the protection results were terrible and the taxes very high the contractors could not have a libertarian objection to it. But why on Earth suppose that the state would offer people protection as good as "it was reasonable to imagine any private agency could?" All the libertarian economic arguments for the inefficiency of state monopoly provision of anything, including law and order, still apply. Where are the answers to the specific efficiency criticisms of the state as provider here?[2] They are simply and completely ignored. So there is nothing more for me to respond to. Maybe Conway thinks that he mainly needs to overcome absolute libertarian rights, and so can simply use such a thought experiment. If so, that is a big error.

Conway then continues with the modified supposition that, instead, "the vast majority of a society wish to affiliate politically with one another and have their rights protected and common good advanced by the same agency. Then, it would seem that part of the terms of membership of that society include a willingness on the part of its members to accept the political obligations attendant upon being a member of that society" (p. 65). Now, we need to distinguish "society" and 'state' here—which Conway appears to conflate. Society as such is a free and spontaneous association of people. A state is an organisation that proactively, in all known cases, imposes control on persons and property within some geographical boundaries. The "vast majority" (or even tiny minority) of a society has every right contractually to set up a 'state' over themselves ("affiliate politically ...") in the way imagined. But that state is a separate organisation from even their part of society, which is, *ipso facto*, not an organisation. Still less is that state the originally imagined society as a whole. It cannot legitimately impose its rule, or taxes, on those who did not contract in. Thus, by these conflations, Conway appears to have produced an erroneous argument for the legitimate majoritarian setting up of a state.

A strange assertion follows: "Contrary to what libertarians claim, most members of these societies do not consider themselves passively acquiescing victims of injustice at the hands of their states, but as their loyal and patriotic citizens" (p. 66). This view of libertarians cannot be right. Surely most libertarians would agree with me in freely acknowledging that the overwhelming majority of people see the state as fundamentally just and themselves as "loyal and patriotic citizens". That is exactly the practical problem. It is what we are trying to change. We know—following Étienne de la Boéttie (1530-1563), David Hume (1711-1776), and Gustave de Molinari (1819-1912)—that the overall social system ultimately rests on popular support. Only a majoritarian, such as Conway, would think that this fact is somehow sufficient to defend the legitimacy of a state. Libertarians' precise theories can vary somewhat, but we are generally agreed that the state is the foremost destroyer of liberty and general welfare (causing all sorts of problems from mass unemployment to mass murder) through its proactive impositions on people and their property. That most people do not agree is beside the point as regards the truth of this libertarian thesis, but not as regards the possibility of abolishing the state. These two issues need to be kept quite separate to avoid confusion.

An even stranger assertion then follows: "The apparent preference of Rothbard and other libertarians for protection within the conditions of anarchy rather than statehood seems based upon an almost wilful blindness to the amounts of organized evil to which human flesh is all too liable to fall victim" (p. 66). To be clear, "anarchy" here can only mean 'society without a state'. It cannot mean 'society without law and order'. Now, if we wish to consider "organized evil" where do we find the most egregiously heinous examples? Not in any criminal gangs but in virtually any state in history. Mass murder by the state is not rare. Many might assume that state wars are the biggest killer and, in any case, inevitable once one side attacks (so one side might have a *prima facie* claim to be killing in its own defence). But war is nowhere near as big a killer as the death toll exacted when states kill their own subjects. R. J. Rummel calculates that in the twentieth century alone, states murdered nearly 174 million of their own subjects. Rummel states that this is "over four-times those killed in combat in all international and domestic wars during the same years."[3] Thus it seems that the "almost wilful blindness" entirely belongs to statists. Where is there any sound argument or evidence that a society free of these states would be more bloody? Conway merely offers us his commonsense prejudice as a self-evident truth.

The events of 11th September 2001 show, for Conway, that the USA needs to be more vigilant to remain a relatively free society. He dismisses, without direct arguments, the view that the American state's military interventions all over the world and some billions of dollars a year subsidy to Israel (a more precise figure risks being irrelevantly disputed) were the main spurs to the terrorism. As he does not criticise this position properly, as he undoubtedly ought, there is again nothing to which I can reply here. Instead, Conway cites World War Two and asks what would have happened to the USA had the German-state beaten the British and Soviet ones (p. 67). The clear answer is that American lives and wealth would have been preserved and the US world-hegemony curbed. However, the war is often defended—with the benefit of hindsight—as morally necessary in light of what the Nazi German-state was doing to the Jews (although the German-state invasion of Poland was the actual occasion for the UK-state to declare war). So a more useful question might be, what would have happened if the American-state and British-state had early on allowed free immigration, in the libertarian (and classical liberal) manner, instead of eventually declaring war on the German-state? More Jews would have been saved (although it was mainly east European Jews that died, often after choosing not to emigrate when they could have done so)[4] British and American lives and wealth would have been preserved: there is good evidence that Hitler had no desire to attack Britain and the British empire (let alone the USA). The 'thousand-year Reich' might well have fizzled out or been considerably ameliorated after the death of Hitler, quite possibly by assassination, as fast as Spanish fascism faded after Franco. Either there would have been no more Soviet Union without American-state support or it would not have expanded. The mere statement of these views is not supposed to convince. The point is that such counterfactual-history has been much debated and cannot simply be ignored. Conway uncritically adopts the position of the court historians. And is this supposed to defend the death by cowardly bombing of more innocent Afghanistanis than those people who died in the World Trade Center? And also, at a conservative estimate, somewhere around 100,000, so far, killed in Iraq?[5]

We are told that classical liberals have "nationalistic attachments and affiliations" (p. 81). But these "attachments and affiliations" need be no more than patriotism: the love of one's homeland and its people. Even libertarians can and do feel this. Nationalism, however, has a strong tendency to war at the worst of times and economic depredations at the best. Thus nationalism ought to be seen as the enemy of all true patriotism.

Conway sees multinationalism and multiculturalism as threats to liberalism (p. 90). An anarchist can immediately concede that multinationalism, like any nationalism, is a threat to liberalism. And having rival nationalisms in one area is likely to be even worse. Also, the state-imposed multiculturalism that we now have does not allow freedom of association or free speech and introduces new crimes based on race alone; all of which certainly tend to promote conflict. But where is the threat from multiculturalism as such? Apparently the state will be used for exploitation and oppression of and by the various alien cultures, some of which may be highly illiberal in the first place. But what if there were no state to use for this purpose? Then that argument also fails.

Contra Conway, it is entirely illiberal for the state to insist on all learning the national language (pp. 92-3). He suggests that "through fostering or even permitting linguistic apartheid, multiculturalism is sowing the seeds of future disunion and anarchy" (p. 93). 'Apartheid' was state-imposed racial segregation. It is grossly misleading to put this on a par with permitting people to speak different languages. Given that Conway wants the state to force people to learn the 'national language', it would be less inaccurate to say that Conway is advocating 'linguistic inverted-apartheid' (forced linguistic integration). And what is wrong with "disunion"? Why is it a problem if people choose to have completely separate ways of life as long as they do so peacefully? To assume that "anarchy" is undesirable (assuming he means absence of the state, as he ought in this context) is to beg the question. Later Conway states that "false individualism sees only chaos where there has not been deliberate order and design" (96). But this is just how Conway appears to see anarchism. Conway might even mean by 'anarchy' a Hobbesian war of all against all and have in mind such things as strife in the Balkans. If so, he is mistaken to think he can fairly assume this is the obvious and inevitable result of abolishing the state without, in this context, also addressing anarcho-liberal arguments to the contrary.

If any nation-state is legitimate then Israel is, says Conway, and particular Israeli-state crimes do not invalidate this general legitimacy. However, if, as some see it, repeated land theft is the particular crime that allowed the Israelis to become a majority, then Conway's assertion is dubious by his own standards. The anarchist can offer, at best, vacuous agreement: because no nation-state is legitimate, Israel isn't. That aside, how can liberalism be squared with the assertion that "the USA is to be applauded rather than condemned for having always continued to support Israel" (183). "The USA" here is not the people but the state that extorts money from the people it rules over and gives it to the Israeli-state (though giving it to the Israeli subjects would not be much better). How is that liberal? And how is the purpose of the expenditures really liberal either? The USA-state has provided uncritical support for the Israeli-state over the years. This policy has clearly undercut the broader interests of the American people. It is not clear that it is really in the interests of the Israeli people either.

One naturally suspects that Conway's support for nationalism has at least something to do with his support for Israel. It is irrelevant to the soundness of his arguments that this might be so, of course. But it should be relevant to defend anarchy in Israel. Immediately, there would not be an Israeli-state (though people might individually still choose to call their state-less homeland 'Israel'). And the Israeli-state is what Israel's enemies object to most, not just what that state does. But then neither would the Israeli-state be able to do anything and so that objection would also fall away. The great fear of supporters of the Israeli-state is that the surrounding states would then simply invade to set up a Palestinian-state, probably slaughtering large numbers of people in the process; and possibly expelling any remaining cultural Israelis thereafter. This fear is based on the mistaken assumption that only a state can offer serious defence against bellicose aggressor states. But to abandon the state is not to abandon all one's armaments and armies. It is just to make sure that these are financed by voluntary contributions and manned by volunteers, so unlikely to extend beyond what people feel is really needed to protect themselves. The fact that there would be no Israeli-state, that the culturally Israeli areas would still be mightily armed but now only for defence, and that this defence would probably target any particular foreign individuals (including by offering a tempting bounty) responsible for any attack, would make any aggression against the culturally Israeli areas *far less* likely than it is now[6] If both sides to any historical disputes agreed to arbitrations on a private-property basis (not 'Israel' versus a potential 'Palestine') by a genuinely independent court system set up for the purpose, then that would also be a great move towards resolving the situation. But none of this is at all likely until people come both to prefer peace (wars are often popular with the majority of the public, despite public demonstrations against them by statist-liberal minorities) and to realise that the state's 'national defence' is not the solution but itself the main problem. And I do not predict that this is likely any time soon. I am more concerned, in this essay at least, with the ultimately correct theoretical answer than with any immediately practical suggestions.

In sum, from a libertarian (and partly even classical liberal) perspective, I am inclined to think the relevant parts of Conway's book might have been improved if he had taken advantage of some of the more radical libertarian critics known to him. But otherwise the book reads very well and I would recommend it as going in the right direction as far as most people are concerned.

Notes

[1] See his *The Ultimate Resource 2* (Princeton: Princeton University Press, 1996).
[2] For instance, see Bruce L. Benson, *The Enterprise of Law: Justice without the State* (San Francisco: Pacific Research Institute for Public Policy, 1990).
[3] http://www.hawaii.edu/powerkills/welcome.html. But on Rummel's error that 'democracy' is the best solution to this evil see James Ostrowski's "Does Democracy Promote Peace" (work in progress)
http://www.mises.org/asc/2002/asc8-ostrowski.pdf.
[4] "Although 85,000 Jewish refugees reached the United States between March 1938 and September 1939, this level of immigration was far below the number seeking refuge. At the 1938 Evian Conference, no country except the Dominican Republic was prepared to increase immigration quotas. In 1939, both Cuba and the United States refused to admit over 900 Jewish refugees who had sailed from Hamburg, Germany, on the 'St. Louis.' The ship was forced to return to Europe where, ultimately, many of the passengers perished in concentration or extermination camps." From the section on Refugees posted at: http://www.ushmm.org/wlc/en/
[5] Les Roberts, Riyadh Lafta, Richard Garfield, Jamal Khudhairi, and Gilbert Burnham, "Mortality before and after the 2003 Invasion of Iraq: Cluster Sample Survey", *The Lancet* [vol. 364, 2004, pp1857-64].
http://www.thelancet.com/journal/
[6] For essays on this key anarcho-liberal issue of defence, see Hans-Hermann Hoppe, ed., *The Myth of National Defense: Essays on the Theory and History of Security Production* (Auburn, Al.: Ludwig von Mises Institute, 2003).
http://www.mises.org/etexts/defensemyth.pdf

27) A Plague on Both your Statist Houses: a Commentary Concerning Justice

(From *Simple Justice*, by Charles Murray, et al., 2005.)

Why Libertarian Restitution Beats State-Retribution and State-Leniency

Charles Murray describes himself as a libertarian, most notably in his short book, *What it Means to be a Libertarian*.[1] He might more accurately have described himself as having libertarian tendencies. My reading of "Simple Justice" is that the views it espouses are far more traditionalist than libertarian. Neither traditionalist state-retribution nor modernist state-leniency is libertarian. Nor does either provide as just or efficient a response to crime as does libertarian restitution, including restitutive retribution. Here, I shall respond directly only to Murray's views, rather than also deal with state-leniency. This is because I accept Murray's thesis, without endorsing his specific arguments for it, that state-leniency is disastrous as a response to crimes against persons and their justly acquired property.

It is shocking and disgusting to see states today give violators of persons and property the upper hand, while they commit their crimes, throughout the judicial procedure after apprehension and during their trials, and in their final sentencing upon being convicted. The offensiveness of this country's criminal justice system is compounded by the gross inefficiency of state policing here. However, to agree with Murray about the injustice and inefficiency of the current way of dealing with crime is about as far as a libertarian can really go. In commenting on Murray's paper, I shall outline a radical and genuinely progressive libertarian option. In so doing, I recognise, and make no apology for the fact, that I stand at the extreme end of the libertarian spectrum.

Who needs the state?

According to those who occupy my preferred end of the libertarian spectrum, states serve no useful purposes, including the maintenance of law and order, that could not be achieved more effectively and justly by private and purely voluntary agencies and associations, created and maintained out of the uncoerced actions of ordinary private individuals acting only from self-interest and the dictates of their consciences.[2]

Throughout, I use 'libertarian' in this extreme sense, although there are also minimal-state libertarians. I shall begin by briefly outlining my own libertarian conception of crime and of the way in which it should be treated, with which even most radical libertarians may disagree, and without offering very much by way of clarification or criticism of it.[3]

The origins of law may be traced to anarchically evolved, and ever-evolving, enforceable rules of conduct specifying how people must behave to avoid aggressing against the persons or justly acquired property of others.[4] Acts that intentionally or recklessly aggress against the persons or property of others—and which thereby tend to add indignity and fear—constitute the only 'crimes' there are in the libertarian sense of that word. That there are no real victimless crimes—for instance, producing and selling state-banned medications or recreational drugs—is a key libertarian tenet that Murray fails even to mention.

In the libertarian view, there is no necessary connection between law and crime, on the one hand, and what a state decides to command or forbid by way of conduct, on the other. A state may forbid conduct not at all criminal in the libertarian sense, and it may permit conduct that is criminal. Indeed, from the libertarian perspective, states themselves notoriously authorise and engage in forms of criminal conduct, most notably taxation (systematic extortion) and aggressive war (mass murder). Note that this evolved-law thesis asserts not merely that such state 'law' and activity is immoral, but that it is not really law or legal at all. A type of conduct no more becomes legal or illegal simply because the state says so, than it becomes moral or immoral because it does. Nor does anyone's command become law simply because he has the power to enforce it.

Wherever a genuine crime has taken place, in the libertarian sense of the term, then there is some victim of it whose person or justly acquired property has been proactively imposed on in some way by another person and who, in consequence, enjoys against that perpetrator of the crime a just claim to full restitution for the disvalue sustained as a result of its perpetration—in principle, at least, for it might not always be practical or possible to extract it. Thus, libertarian criminal law and civil law overlap. All crimes require restitution, but not all legal restitution is owed because of a crime. Perpetrators of crime owe their victims, as restitution, more than whatever would fully compensate for whatever proximate damage, or loss, that their victims suffer to their person or property, including any feelings of shock or fear they suffer as a result of these crimes. In addition, perpetrators of crime owe their victims restitution for the additional risk to which they put them that they might not be able to recover any restitution because their assailant manages to escape conviction. I call this latter variable the 'risk-multiplier'.

The risk-multiplier

For example, if there is only a one in ten chance that perpetrators of a given kind of crime are apprehended and convicted, then full restitution to victims of it involves the perpetrators having to cede to their victims something of equal value to the value of the proximate loss each suffers to person or property and multiplied by ten. This is precisely what victims require to receive from their assailants to take account of the risk that was imposed on them.[5] Only to require criminals to make restitution for whatever proximate damage they cause their victims would mean they are allowed to impose on their victims, without having to make any restitution for it, the often far greater disvalue they cause their victims by the risk that they might escape.[6]

Consider a different kind of case from the risk-multiplier, but one that clarifies the disvalue of imposed risks as such. Suppose someone imposes on your head a game of Russian roulette in which the gun does not fire, although there was a one-in-six chance it might have done. Surely you are owed not just for any fear, etc., to which you were subjected, which, in this instance, forms the proximate damage you were made to suffer, and which might have been relatively small had the episode occurred very suddenly or even without your knowing at the time. You are also owed an additional amount, probably much higher and possibly infinite, that it would be reasonable of you to demand from anyone who sought to impose that risk on you. Similarly, someone caught and convicted of a crime should not be let off having to provide his victim with restitution for the risk he had imposed on him that he might, *ex ante*, have got away with his crime.[7]

Insuring against crime

However, the full debts perpetrators of crime owe their victims in restitution for their crimes are debts the victims might have chosen, in anticipation they might become victims, to 'sell' on to insurance companies through taking out policies against any losses sustained by becoming a victim of such (or any) crimes. Victims might also be able literally to sell the restitution owed them after they have fallen victim to a crime. In either case, victims of crime would acquire against their insurers a claim for a sum that would fully compensate them for any proximate disvalue suffered, but which takes no, or only partial, account of the risk-multiplier. Whether or by how much it did would depend on the precise terms of their contract.

Those who take out such policies might be able to have a guarantee they will receive compensation should they ever fall a victim of crime, even if its perpetrators are never detected. Meanwhile, their insurance companies will have acquired from their clients a claim, should they become victims of crime, against their assailants for recovery of the full debt they owe their clients. This full debt they owe includes what is generated by the risk-multiplier. The difference between what companies pay out to their clients in compensation for becoming victims of crime and what the companies thereby become owed by its perpetrators provides them with the inducement to take over these debts that criminals, in the first instance, owe their victims.

Competing private agencies are far more likely to be able to catch and prosecute genuine criminals without becoming corrupted in the process than are state institutions, which maintain monopolies in this domain by aggressive violence. Moreover, competing private insurance companies are more likely than states to ensure that victims of crime receive quick and adequate compensation. The large amounts owing as a result of the risk-multiplier might be thought to create the moral hazard of inviting fabrication of evidence, whether by individuals or institutions. However, it must be remembered that the risk-multiplier also applies in cases of any large sums fraudulently claimed. In addition, most claims will be sold on to insurance companies, which stand to lose all custom if found fraudulent in this way if not simply wiped out immediately by having to pay any risk-multiplier debt.

Restitutive retribution

If mere financial compensation were the only form in which restitution could be demanded by victims, then people who wished to commit crime would effectively be able to purchase a licence to do so. Should victims prefer, they should be able to obtain 'restitutive retribution'.[8] This is exacted by criminals being made to suffer as much personal injury or pain as they caused their victims magnified by any risk-multiplier. If you twist my arm, as though it were your property to use as you wish and in doing so break it, you thereby cede me a reciprocal right to break yours, or else for me to have it broken by an agent acting for me. This might look like retribution pure and simple. Where is the literal restitution, or restoration, in my breaking your arm? However, suppose the restitution owing me in monetary terms is £100,000. Should I prefer to take some fraction of that sum in the form of some reciprocal treatment of you, then that is simply how I choose to spend that much of the restitution I am owed. Alternatively, I might prefer to take all my compensation in money and buy a car instead, but that would not 'restore' my arm to not being broken either. You cannot complain that I am *proactively imposing* on you or imposing to a greater degree than you had imposed on me. Proactive impositions and reactions in excess of the risk-multiplier are all that this libertarian theory disallows.

From a libertarian perspective, therefore, the key deficiency in Murray's account is the false dichotomy it poses between, on the one hand, retribution in the sense of punishment and, on the other hand, leniency. The libertarian position, by contrast, is one that embodies restitution for crime, where this is understood as criminals having to repay their victims amounts equal in value to whatever overall losses they have caused—although, as we have seen, victims may choose to obtain restitution in a retributive way. I should add that Murray also fails to distinguish, and then reconcile, deontological and consequentialist arguments for retribution.

In none of the seven hypothetical scenarios that Murray offers to test the moral proclivities of his readers (pp. 7-8) does he include among the possible options an explicitly libertarian response. If, in all the relevant hypothetical scenarios save the last, restitution is put in place of punishment, a libertarian can happily answer '3' to all the questions that Murray asks about them. The final hypothetical scenario concerns the legitimacy of forcibly injecting a criminal-suspect with a truth drug. In this case, to force a suspect not yet found guilty to take such a drug, without at least his having previously entered into some contractual obligation to submit to one upon suspicion, is itself a case of proactively imposing upon someone, and thus a crime in the libertarian sense. Moreover, when libertarian restitution is substituted for punishment, it becomes difficult to see why opting for '3' in any of the other cases qualifies as being "tough", the adjective Murray uses to describe the attitudes of those likely to choose that option. What is so tough about thinking that victims of crime qualify for receiving from their assailants full restitution and ought to receive it, if often only indirectly via insurance companies?

Is the state a community?

Murray claims "[t]he primal function of a system of justice is to depersonalise revenge ... [T]he individual will take his complaint to the community. In return, the community will exact the appropriate retribution; partly on behalf of the wronged individual, but also to express the community's moral values" (pp. 18-19). What is said here seems wrong on many levels. Justice does not have an 'essence' or "primary function" that simply needs to be cited to succeed thereby in refuting all competing conceptions of justice. If retribution is superior to restitution, Murray needs to argue for that thesis. Individual victims of crime may need the support of others, but why should they be entitled to receive it from "the community"? Murray appears to use this term as a euphemism for the state. However, whereas the state is an organisation (and, in the eyes of libertarians, a criminal one), a community is not. Nor is a community a moral agent, so it has no "moral values." Only individuals have these. Why cannot private agencies assist wronged persons better than can states, as has been argued by many libertarian theorists, not least by Bruce Benson?[9]

On behalf of his position, Murray cites the Kantian thought-experiment that asks whether a murderer should be executed if his execution served no purpose other than 'pure justice' (p. 19). Kant and Murray say he should be. Libertarians say the correct answer is to be found in the victim's legal-defence contract, or in his will, or in his known or likely opinion, or in the decision of his heirs or other relevantly assigned persons, although I doubt many would want to let the murderer off. It is not up to "the community"—that is, the state—to decide.

Murray is similarly wrong when later on he explicitly states that victims "do not have the moral right to abrogate the community's obligation to punish wrong behaviour" (p. 20). In the event that a victim of some crime genuinely wishes to receive no restitution from his assailant, then, assuming there has been no intimidation of the victim by the criminal etc., that should be his or her choice, however foolish most other people might find it. In a sense, the victim retroactively consents to undergoing whatever the criminal has inflicted on him. In these circumstances, whoever exacts "retribution" on behalf of that victim or "the community" *initiates* a crime against the aggressor who has been forgiven by his victim. Such injustices are the sorts of thing that typically occur when statists attempt to take the law into their own hands in the name of "the community" or society. From a libertarian point of view, however, there is nothing unjust in people choosing to ban, boycott or berate anyone for any reason at all, provided in so acting they proceed in accordance with private-property rules. Hence, provided they conform with these rules, people may take such action against anyone whose behaviour they regard as despicable, although whoever it is might have escaped and be able to escape successful prosecution for acting as he has done. For instance, many might for such a reason choose to ban someone from their private property and policing companies might even refuse to protect such a person.

Murray explains the "core tenets" of retributive justice as follows:

> The necessary and sufficient justification for punishing criminals is that they did something for which they deserve punishment. 'Something' refers to the behaviours that society has defined as offences. 'Deserve' means that the offenders are culpable—

morally responsible. *Society not only has the right but the duty to punish culpable offenders.* (p. 20. Emphases in original.)

Again, from a libertarian perspective, what Murray claims here is open to all sorts of question. What right has "society" to define what does and does not count as an offence, when all that is here meant by "society" is some state run according to the rules of elected oligarchs? It is, objectively, an offence, as the opposite of a defence, for anyone knowingly to impose proactively on the person or justly acquired property of someone else. If people merely defend themselves or their property against such impositions, then they are not guilty of any offences against anyone. The state itself commits crimes when it attempts to impose on people things that conflict with protecting persons and their property. How and why should anyone be "culpable" if they seek to evade such arbitrary impositions? The state is not "society", a term which denotes the free and spontaneous association of people. Nor has a state the right to punish anyone, even if a victim wants it to do so. For the opportunity-cost of its so doing is to exclude the possibility of the superior market system that would operate without the state's extortion of resources through taxation and inflation of the money supply, the two principal sources of the state's revenue.

Who needs judges?

Why should it be supposed, as Murray appears to, that, in all criminal cases, there is need of "jurors" or "judges"? Murray only supposes this because he is thinking entirely within the traditionalist statist framework of law and order. It is hard in advance to know what different methods of securing and administering criminal justice would evolve were only the market allowed to operate here. On-the-spot payments for relatively minor crimes, as even the present British government has recently suggested for shoplifting although not as restitution, need not be either inefficient or an easy option, especially given the risk-multiplier element.

In defending the admissibility in court of the past criminal record of an accused on trial, something with which I cannot disagree, Murray interestingly suggests that "[d]ivinely accurate retributive justice would not punish for the one burglary out of dozens when the burglar got caught, but for the aggregate harm that the burglar has done" (p. 25). This is effectively what criminals are being asked to provide as restitution when what they are computed as owing takes into account the risk-multiplier. Its extraction would feel to the criminal as though he were being punished for all the times he was not caught as well. Moreover, what the criminal will be deemed to owe for his crime will, through using the risk-multiplier, often be a lot more severe than state punishment currently is. Only the exaction of this form of restitution maximises the chances that "crime does not pay", which is Murray's expressed desire in his final end-note. In principle, it will, typically, not be worth committing any crime because its potential benefits will be at least negated by its potential losses, and any other efforts and expenses will make it even less attractive. We should certainly see the crime level drop back again, and to far lower levels than obtained even in the 1950s to which Murray likes to hark back. We would only see the risk-multiplier fall if proportionally more criminals were brought to book.

Like many traditionalists, Murray is keen on prison. He writes, "[i]n modern England, the only authentic punishment for modern felonies is imprisonment" (p. 25). Prison is indeed a serious punishment. But it is both Draconian and unnecessarily expensive for the most part, while being too lenient in extreme cases. Unless someone poses so great a risk to others that he is likely to do more damage than he could ever pay in restitution, or else he refuses to pay restitution (non-contractual bankruptcy cannot be an option), there is no need for his incarceration. Such extreme cases are relatively few and far between and will be all the more so once criminals see that full risk-multiplier restitution will be enforced. In any case, since, in a libertarian world, prisoners will be obliged to pay their way in prison, being obliged to work there if they want to be fed, there is no need to worry about the expense of maintaining them whilst incarcerated in private prisons. However, for many lesser criminals, mere electronic tagging would at most be necessary or else some other, more inventive, option that only competition is likely to evolve efficiently. And these would provide more cost-effective and more humane alternatives to prison.

In the small minority of cases in which huge debts are owed that are unlikely to be paid by ordinary work, then extreme measures must be taken to recover them. These would still not be punishment but remain the enforcement of restitution. What I am proposing might sound harsh. But the only alternative is to allow the guilty to get away with their crimes against the innocent, which is surely harsher and completely unjust. Sometimes, a crime will be too great for full restitution to be possible, either in terms of property damage (malicious computer viruses often cause this) or personal damage, even a single murder, let alone bombing innocent civilians for political reasons. In these cases, we shall at least have done the best we can.

Overall, Murray's traditionalist-retribution might be less bad than is the existing modernist-leniency that offers even less by way of just and efficient deterrence. However, in arguing for it, Murray entirely overlooks a third option more just, progressive and efficient than either. This is the way of dealing with crime through enforcing libertarian-restitution as the appropriate response to it. Murray must have read enough libertarian literature to be aware of this third option. It is a pity he chose not to consider it in his essay.[10]

Notes

[1] New York: Broadway Books, 1997.
[2] The two rightly celebrated introductions to this ideology are David D. Friedman, *The Machinery of Freedom: Guide to a Radical Capitalism* (1973; 2nd ed., La Salle, Ill.: Open Court, 1989) and Murray N. Rothbard, *For a New Liberty: The Libertarian Manifesto* (1973; rev. ed., New York: Macmillan Co., 1978).
[3] For a more detailed and philosophical exposition of the position taken here see J. C. Lester, 'Libertarian Rectification: Restitution, Retribution, and the Risk-Multiplier', *Journal of Value Inquiry* 34, no. 2-3 (2000): 287-297, or J. C. Lester, *Escape from Leviathan: Liberty, Welfare and Anarchy Reconciled* (Basingstoke: Macmillan; New York: St Martin's Press, 2000), 108-120.
[4] F. A. Hayek has famously distinguished spontaneously evolved law from state legislation in his *Law, Legislation and Liberty* (London: Routledge & Kegan Paul, [1973-79], 1982). But as a classical liberal, rather than a libertarian, he thinks that state legislation can be a useful supplement. See also Bruno Leoni's *Freedom and the Law* (1961; expanded 3rd ed., Indianapolis: Liberty Fund, 1991).
[5] All victims of this type of crime have a claim of this sort, but if more than one in ten aggressors starts being caught then the risk-multiplier eventually comes down in proportion.
[6] I suspect there are difficulties with my current formulation of the risk-multiplier but my intuition is that some consistent version of it is possible and correct.
[7] During the course of a crime, the risk-multiplier restitution that would be owed if the aggressor escapes means the victim can retaliate up to that value. It will be very approximate at the time, of course, but it means that the victim has clear leeway to be more violent than the criminal (even, in restitutive retribution, as the criminal is fleeing: this might be seen as a more just version of the "outlaw" view that Murray defends).
[8] Here I agree with Bruce L. Benson, and disagree with some other libertarians, that there is room in libertarian restitution for retribution (i.e., that restitution may be taken in the form of retribution). See Bruce Lowell Benson, 'Restitution in Theory and Practice', *Journal of Libertarian Studies* 12, no. 1 (1996): 75–97.
[9] For instance, see Bruce L. Benson, *The Enterprise of Law: Justice without the State* (San Francisco: Pacific Research Institute for Public Policy, 1990).
[10] This essay is far clearer than it otherwise would have been thanks to critical responses from Mark Brady, David Conway, David Goldstone and David McDonagh.

28) Smoking and Libertarianism: a reply to Amartya Sen

(Unpublished letter to the *Financial Times*, 2007.)

Dear Sir, re "Unrestrained smoking is a libertarian half-way house", by Amartya Sen (February 12, 2007). Liberty is not Professor Sen's forté. Some libertarian corrections:

1. Any harm from "passive smoking" is self-inflicted when one is voluntarily on premises where smoking is allowed by the owner. Therefore, there is no libertarian case at all for restricting it.

2. Harm to others is not a "necessary justification" for interfering with liberty. We may harm others with their consent (such as in a boxing match).

3. No "habit-forming behaviour" ever "restricts the freedom of the same person in the future." Firstly, this has nothing to do with having our freedom (or liberty) restricted by the interference of others, which is what libertarianism is about. Second, there is nothing to stop us from choosing to put up with any temporary withdrawal symptoms.

4. John Stuart Mill was simply mistaken to write of someone's selling himself into slavery that, "it is not freedom to be allowed to alienate his freedom". If someone chooses to alienate any of his freedom by contract, or even completely by suicide, then clearly that is his decision and it would be an invasion of his liberty to stop him. (Though comparing acquiring the habit of smoking with a slave contract is absurd.)

5. There is no such moral agent or organisation as "society" that can judge smokers. Professor Sen can mean only agents of the state. And the NHS is not a "public resource", it is a state resource. These are euphemisms for unlibertarian collectivism.

6. The revenue from tobacco taxation is many times the amount that the NHS allegedly spends on smoking-related health problems. So it is the non-smokers who are being subsidised at the coerced expense of the smokers.

The "half-way house erected by an inadequate assessment of the demands of liberty" would, if completed, give smokers much more liberty than now, and certainly more than Professor Sen would like. However, if private health insurance replaced the disastrous universal "free at the point of consumption" NHS, then we might expect smokers to think twice when they see the immediate and ongoing financial costs to themselves of their behaviour.

Yours sincerely,

J C Lester

29) The Political Compass and Why Libertarianism is not Right-Wing

(From *Journal of Social and Evolutionary Systems*, vol. 17, no. 3 [1994], pp. 231-41.)

Abstract

The political distinction between left and right remains ideologically muddled. This was not always so, but an immediate return to the pristine usage is impractical. Putting a theory of social liberty to one side, this essay defends the interpretation of left-wing as personal-choice and right-wing as property-choice. This allows an axis that is north/choice (or state-free) and south/control (or state-ruled). This Political Compass clarifies matters without being tendentious or too complicated. It shows that what is called 'libertarianism' is north-wing. A quiz gives the reader's Political Compass reading.

Pristine clarity and modern confusion

The modern political left/right division is too crude to accommodate many important political positions in a way that makes any sense. Libertarianism (or extreme classical liberalism) is sometimes placed, often implicitly or vaguely, somewhere on the extreme right. But can we say whether it ought to be to the right or left of other 'right-wing' ideologies? How are we to indicate the extreme tolerance of personal choice (as regards drug use and consenting sexual practices, for instance) that libertarianism entails but which is not normally thought of as being right-wing?

Samuel Brittan sees clearly the confusion in the modern left and right (though assuming a libertarian view of liberty):

> The dilemma of the [classical] liberal is that while Conservatives now use the language of individual freedom, they apply this only—if at all—to domestic economic questions. They are the less libertarian of the two parties—despite individual exceptions—on all matters of personal and social conduct, and are much the more hawk-like in their attitude to 'foreign affairs'. Labour, on the other hand, has liberal instincts on foreign affairs and personal conduct,

but is perversely blind to the claims of economic liberty, which is distrusted as a capitalist rationalisation. (Brittan 1968, p. 131)

The original political meanings of 'left' and 'right' have changed since their origin in the French estates general in 1789. There the people sitting on the left could be viewed as more or less anti-statists with those on the right being state-interventionists of one kind or another. In this interpretation of the pristine sense, libertarianism was clearly at the extreme left-wing.[1] This sense lasted up to as late as 1848, with Frédéric Bastiat sitting on the left in the National Assembly. In Britain, it was the Fabians in particular who adopted old Tory ideas, asserted that they were more to the left than free trade, and labelled them as 'socialism' (Rothbard 1979). In the wake of the Fabians the old left and right has been muddled. It might be thought that there is now a swing back to the old labels. For instance, the Russians now call the Communists 'right-wing'. But it seems that they are mainly following the West in using 'right-wing' as a pejorative.

A return to this original meaning would fail to make important distinctions that currently dominate political thought. One problem would be that any existing left and right groups with mirrored policies of state intervention in personal and property matters (say, 40/60 and 60/40) would, confusingly, find themselves at the same point on the right-wing of the political line. The modern left-right view is also extremely popular: virtually everyone has some conception of what it means. People have often tried and failed to show what is wrong with it and how it can be replaced (some examples follow). That they have failed is a sign of its stability. These two facts make it impractical to convince people of the virtue of an immediate return to the old distinction.

So a single political line provides no solutions to these problems. As a result, it is sometimes suggested that the political array is better viewed as a circle in which the extremes meet: the extreme left and the extreme right differing more in rhetoric than in reality.[2] There is undoubtedly some truth in the idea about differing more in rhetoric than reality. Hitler's Germany and Stalin's Soviet Union have often been taken as extremes of right and left. But behind the political labels they look practically identical rather than opposite. People often admit the Hitler-Stalin similarity, yet that does not stop them thinking that Stalin is left and Hitler is right and that the market must *somehow* be on the right (being the opposite of communism).[3] Hence, in their confusion, they can only come up with a circle (figure 1).

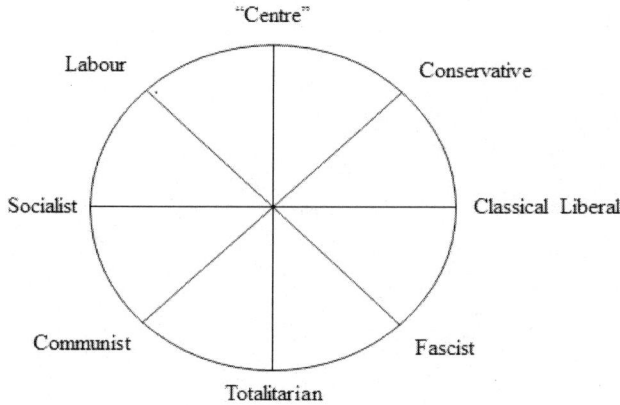

Figure 1

It is hard to see how the political circle has better real explanatory value than the political line. The circle fails to distinguish the distinctively left and right elements both from each other and from other political elements. Perhaps this is because the idea of a political circle is not inspired by a desire to clarify matters but by a dogmatic delight in a paradox that seems to make all extreme political views inherently absurd. But the circle may be a useful first stage for illustrating the confusion in the left/right view, for the paradox does not withstand serious investigation.

Having an axis to grind

One idea that makes some sense of this confusion, or conflation, is David Nolan's diagrammatical distinction between economic and personal liberty based on the empirical work of professors William Maddox and Stuart Lilie (1984). Nolan puts both types of liberty in the same diagram along two axes. But in my version I use the more neutral term 'choice', to be contrasted with (state) 'control'. I also prefer 'property' as being slightly clearer than 'economic' (figure 2).

Arguments for Liberty

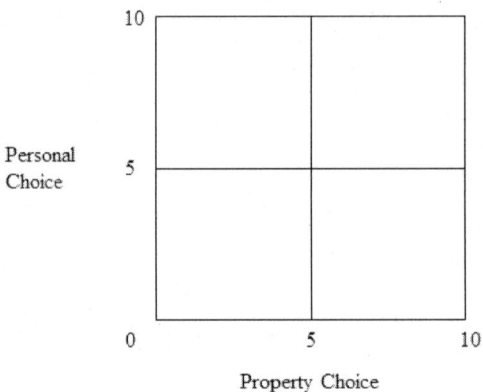

Figure 2

In figure 2, libertarians and classical liberals then find themselves in the top right-hand corner. Authoritarians, including paternalists, are in the bottom left-hand square. Fascism[4] is in the extreme bottom left-hand corner, being the very opposite of libertarianism. 'Left-wingers' are somewhere in the top-left square, with left-wing (anti-money and anti-private property) 'anarchists' in the extreme top left-hand corner. 'Right-wingers', possibly with certain religious fanatics in the corner, are somewhere in the bottom right square.

So perhaps it is a clarificatory caricature to view modern right-wingers as personal state-controllers and left-wingers as property state-controllers. The contrasting distinction is between control and choice (no state-control) over both categories. The clarity of these distinctions enables us to avoid Kedourie's risk of "guilt by association" (1985, pp. 143-147) whereby what is not left is automatically right.

This diagram makes things clearer, but it fails to incorporate the left/right view as simply *left* and *right*. It also fails to give us a felicitous analogous expression for the alternative choice/control distinction. But what if we follow Marshall Fritz (Bergland 1990, pp. 22-23) and rotate the diagram 45 degrees anti-clockwise? (Again, I use my preferred distinctions: figure 3.)

J C Lester

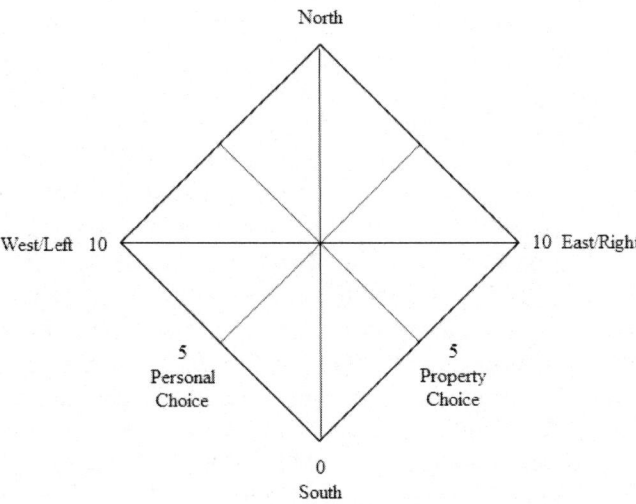

Figure 3

In figure 3, left-wing and right-wing are now to the left and right of the diagram. And we are able to describe the choice/control contrast as 'north-wing' and 'south-wing'. With this distinction, libertarians can position themselves on a Political Compass.[5] The expression 'Political Compass' has long been used, but not much sense of it has been made before as far as I am aware.

In the UK, Jacobs and Worcester have produced a recent attempt to sophisticate the political spectrum that is less successful (1990). The questions they ask often presuppose state-intervention and so the categories arrived at do not allow for a choice/control distinction. Maddox and Lilie share one flaw in their approach. They are too focused on the centre of politics and so cannot make sense of the various extremes. It is misleading to categorise, as Maddox and Lilie do, 18% of Americans as 'libertarians' in any serious sense of the word. Also, their four boxes ignore *other* reasons for wingedness than being Liberal, Libertarian, Populist, or Conservative.[6] Unlike their boxes, the Compass allows for greater precision of direction and degree, and without specifying the particular ideology.

Brittan comes back to left and right in a later book (1973). He quotes the conclusion in *Political Change in Britain*[7] that most people "have wholly atomistic responses to the issues of politics" (p. 356). Though he notes that "statistical psychologists have found significant, although moderate, correlations between views on different issues which enable them to locate 'opinion clusters'" (p. 358). So Brittan gives up the attempt to clarify left and right in the way he did in his earlier book. He sees the search for independent dimensions as mistaken, and concludes that "what different attitudes and individuals, who are characterised as left or right ... have in common are ... 'family resemblances'" (p. 363).

He then gives a list of beliefs "a sufficient combination" of which "will justify the label 'left-wing' in a broader sense than mere proneness to vote Labour" (p. 363). He later gives a breakdown for Conservative political attitudes (p. 366). What he apparently fails to see, or fails to see the significance of, is that the left-wing views are overwhelmingly about state-control in property matters with choice in personal matters, and that the other list is the opposite. This is what sorts out the modern left and right; and this also suggests the single alternative choice/control scale. Having values that fit better on that scale enables us to avoid the crude view that "people are inconsistent", as Maddox and Lilie observe (1984, p. 33), when they do not fit along left and right.

Instead, Brittan tries to make sense of these views by suggesting labels that qualify which kind of left or right is under discussion. But this discourages clear extremes at odds with the general left/right scale. In particular, it discourages something that Brittan says he would value: "a return to a party division in which one side puts together, in Cobdenite fashion, freedom in all its aspects and non-intervention overseas" (1973, p. 371). But he fears that "if the authoritarian party happened to be in power for the greater part of the time, the outlook for freedom would be dim..." (p. 372). It appears that his one-dimensional approach prevents him from seeing that the whole political consensus can simply move northwards so that both, or all, main parties would opt for less state control.

A simpler diagram

The previous diagram is more complicated than is necessary to convey the basic idea. A simpler diagram (figure 4) is possible, taking the clue from the earlier Samuel Brittan (1968, pp. 88-89)[8]: a single vertical choice/control axis can form a cross with the horizontal personal/property choice axis.

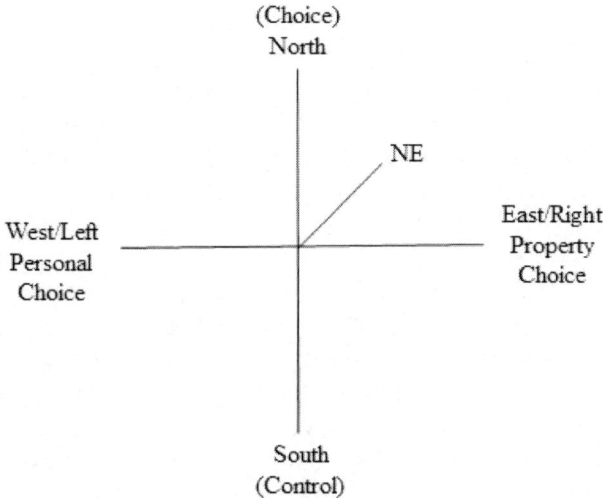

Figure 4

However, though this is an easier idea to grasp, it does not work for plotting political positions directly (it is not itself a Cartesian diagram—and nor are Brittan's—it just looks like one). With the way I have set up the questions below, it will be necessary to work out one's political position on the previous diagram first.

Tendentious axes?

It might be thought that this distinction between personal and property choice is tendentious. I shall consider four criticisms along these lines:

1) The Compass ignores the socio-economic, or class, bias of left and right.

2) The nature of liberty is too controversial to call one Compass point 'libertarian'.

3) The personal/property choice distinction is not coherent.

4) Equally important dimensions could further be distinguished.

1) Is it misleading to ignore the socio-economic, or class, bias of left and right?

The west and east wings are partly stipulative and not intended to capture all that is in the notions of left and right wings. One thing that is ignored is the supposed socio-economic bias of the modern left and right: that there is some slight statistical tendency, in the UK for instance, for Labour to find more votes among the lower socio-economic groups and Tories among the higher.

For one thing, compared to the overall Compass such slight differences are trivial. For another, these differences can be seen as, in practice, reflecting vested interests that cause everyone else to suffer, including those of one's own 'class'. In any case, if the Compass questions produce a three-dimensional bell-shaped distribution curve then that indicates the capture of something socio-ideologically significant, rather than arbitrary groupings of ideas. A failure to be bell-shaped might indicate that the population can more clearly be interpreted along different ideological lines. But this does not in itself show that the Political Compass does not make conceptual sense. Libertarians can still use this idea in order to explain themselves.

2) Can libertarianism be north-wing when 'real liberty' is either to be found in another wing or it is an 'essentially contested concept' (Gallie, 1955)?

If pressed, a libertarian could, in this context at least, concede the libertarian/authoritarian contrast. The choice/control (or state-free/state-controlled) contrast can be accepted as more neutral. He can still preserve the essential north/south distinction that enables his own political position to be more easily understood. This also has the advantage of objectively solving Lilie's philosophical problem of categorising or avoiding issues where the "true libertarian" policy is debatable (Boaz 1986, p. 88).

However, to object to the name 'libertarian' altogether would seem unfair. It is polite debating practice to allow each ideology to be named by its advocates. There are some generally positive connotations to 'conservative' and 'socialist' that it would be equally trivial to complain about.

3) A more radical criticism, sometimes put forward by libertarians, is that the personal/property distinction is not coherent.

These are really two aspects of any human activity: the body is in a broad sense property (or an economic resource); external goods are at some point tied up with someone's personal projects. So, the libertarian might insist, only the north/south (original left/right) axis makes proper sense, and we cannot have the other axis (and so cannot have the Compass).[9]

I see considerable force in this point and so reject the view expressed by Maddox and Lilie that "the extent and nature of government regulation of personal behaviour ... is both *analytically* and empirically distinct from conflict on the economic dimension" (Maddox and Lilie 1984, p. 4, emphasis added). Nevertheless, moral and political distinctions are conventionally made between what are called 'personal' and 'property' issues. I cannot see why these distinctions ought to be entirely ignored because they are indeterminate from a purely conceptual viewpoint. This would be as unfortunate an excuse for continued confusion and dogmatism as is the current insistence on only the modem left/right division. As Brittan puts it,

> Relationships between views on different subjects do not have the authority of logic or mathematics. There are historical, sociological and cultural explanations why a bias towards economic freedom should be combined with an anti-permissive approach to social questions and relatively belligerent external attitudes among Conservatives—just as there are for the combination of state economic intervention, a bias towards freedom in personal behaviour and pacific external attitudes among the Labour Party (1968, p. 142).[10]

The distinction between personal and property choice is conceptually dubious but it is a socio-political reality (somewhat like the mediaeval distinction between ordinary women and witches). And this reality can be illustrated graphically without conceding that it is conceptually coherent. Perhaps by this display people will eventually be brought round to abandoning the current left-right view. But it is a mistake to insist on a choice/control axis without allowing people a clear view of how it relates to the modem left/right view. This is to require an intellectual effort that will be too much for most people, due to lack of real interest in politics, as well as an unnecessarily immediate rejection of their comfortable orthodox distinction.

4) It might also be suggested that we could, in principle, introduce all sorts of theoretical dimensions to complicate the simple left/right one.

I believe that the preceding account captures something very significant politically[11] while not moving too far beyond the popular, simpler distinction to be impractical for general use. Maddox and Lilie show that even 'foreign policy' is also clearly divisible into these four winged approaches (Maddox and Lilie 1984, ch. VII). Samuel Brittan made various attempts to improve on the left/right view (Brittan 1968, pp. 88-89), but none of them appears to have the simplicity and verisimilitude of the view defended here. In the quoted passages, Brittan clearly sees that the personal/property distinction exists, but he does not home in on it as the solution to the mess (perhaps because he is, ideologically, too near the centre of mainstream politics).

In reality, then, it is non-libertarians who are being tendentious if they insist that libertarianism is on the 'extreme right-wing'. This usage is merely a pejorative and an excuse to avoid debate. But now libertarians can, if necessary, practice tit-for-tat by lumping together non-libertarians as undifferentiated 'south-wingers' or 'authoritarians'.

As more people become libertarians, especially more academics and other intellectuals, we might find that their insistence on being 'north-wingers', if they do so insist, gives currency to this interpretation of the Political Compass. The modern political terms 'left' and 'right' will not disappear in a hurry, if at, all, but they do not need to. Though if the Political Compass were to become popular then 'left' might sometimes become 'west' and 'right' become 'east'.

A Political Compass Quiz

Marshall Fritz offers a quiz with only five very general questions for each axis (Bergland 1990, pp. 22-23). The following quiz has ten questions each. These questions are still relatively few and selective. They might fail to place some readers in the proper area.[12] They are roughly in ascending order of extremity, from a conventional viewpoint, of anti-statism. They have been thought up both to clarify the general idea of the Political Compass and to elucidate the nature of the libertarian (choice or state-free) north-wing.

Some questions might seem to be partly relevant to the opposite category. To some extent this is because what are roughly distinguishable as personal and property aspects are contingently bound together in certain issues. But this is also because of the truth of the criticism that the distinction is conceptually dubious.

To give an absolute position on figure 3, and thereby the Compass, give yourself one point on the appropriate axis for each 'Yes' answer (or a fraction of a point to the extent that you agree).

Personal Choice Questions

1) Should people be allowed to follow their own religions in peace and privacy?

2) Should women be allowed contraception and abortions?

3) Should all consenting, private, adult sexual acts be legal?

4) Should all state censorship be abolished?

5) Should employers be allowed to discriminate on any basis they like?

6) Should all drugs be legal?

7) Should all voluntary human sports, no matter how violent, be legal?

8) Should crimes be seen as only against individuals, or private institutions, who are due restitution from the criminals?

9) Should the few political figures responsible for a war be targeted rather than civilians and conscripts?

10) Should state immigration controls be replaced by private-property controls on entry?

Property Choice Questions

1) Should the state stop using taxes to subsidise art and entertainment?

2) Should the state stop using taxes to subsidise industries?

3) Should all state barriers to free trade be abolished?

4) Should people acquire their education from the market or charity instead of by taxation and state intervention?

5) Should voluntary insurance and charity replace state welfare?

6) Should the state's coercive monopoly of money be abolished?

7) Should all roads and streets be privately owned and regulated?

8) Should private ownership be allowed to deal with environmental problems?

9) Should all taxation stop because it is extortion?

10) Should the state's coercive monopoly of law and its enforcement be replaced by competing protection agencies?

Notes

[1] However, nothing about the suggested Political Compass depends on this interpretation being true.
[2] An interesting attempt to make sense of this from a libertarian viewpoint is Jerome Tucille (1970, p. 38). There libertarianism is placed as more extreme than fascism and communism. I cannot see how this really clarifies matters, despite the accompanying explanation.
[3] In Britain, the Revolutionary Communist Party (or at least one RCP debater at the LSE) put Hitler and Stalin on the far right, but themselves, Lenin, and classical liberals on the left. If they mean that we are all anti-authoritarian *in principle* then that is a return to the old labels (in principle—but we have a considerable factual dispute about what is anti-authoritarian in practice).
[4] As Z. Sternhell puts it in *The Blackwell Encyclopaedia of Political Thought*'s entry on 'fascism', "Totalitarianism is the very essence of fascism, and fascism is without question the purest example of totalitarian ideology" (Miller 1987, p. 150). He quotes Mussolini's definition of fascism: "Everything in the state, nothing against the state, nothing outside the state."
[5] "Political map" is the expression Marshal Fritz uses.
[6] Liberal (for personal freedom [+PF] and for government intervention in economic affairs [+GE]); libertarian (+PF, -GE); populist (-PF, +GE); conservative (-PF, -GE).
[7] Butler and Stokes (1969), *Political Change in Britain*, Macmillan, London.
[8] Who, in turn, modified the original idea of Eysenck's psychological tough-minded/tender-minded distinction (1963).
[9] This was the major criticism of David McDonagh in correspondence. It is apparently implied in Hayek's view that "To be controlled in our economic pursuits means to be ... controlled in everything" (Hayek 1976, p. 68).
[10] Brittan continues: "But these combinations are not part of the permanent order of things. At least as good a case can be made for putting together in Cobdenite fashion economic and personal freedom and non-intervention overseas."
[11] As Brittan shows is true in the UK, in both cited books, and the work of Maddox and Lilie bears this out for the USA.
[12] My interest being primarily philosophical, I set aside detailed empirical refinements. It is probably clearer to plot ideologies and not political personalities (as do Brittan and, to a lesser extent, Maddox and Lilie).

References

Bergland, D. (1990), *Libertarianism in One Lesson*, Orpheus Publications, Costa Mesa, CA.

Boaz, D. ed. (1986), *Left, Right and Babyboom: America's New Politics*, Cato Institute, Washington.
Brittan, S. (1968), *Left or Right: the Bogus Dilemma*, Secker and Warburg, London.
Brittan, S. (1973), *Capitalism and the Permissive Society*, Macmillan, London.
Butler and Stokes (1969), *Political Change in Britain*, Macmillan, London.
Eysenck, H. (1963), *The Psychology of Politics*, Routledge, London.
Gallie, W. (1956), "Essentially Contested Concepts" in *Proceedings of the Aristotelian Society*, 56, pp. 167-198.
Hayek, F. (1976 [1944]), *The Road to Serfdom*, Routledge, London and Henley.
Jacobs, E. and Worcester, R. (1990), *We British: Britain Under the MORIscope*, Weidenfeld and Nicholson, London.
Kedourie, E. (1985), *The Crossman Confessions and Other Essays in Politics, History and Religion*, Mansell Publishing, London.
Maddox, W. and Lilie, S. (1984), *Beyond Liberal and Conservative: Reassessing the Political Spectrum*, Cato Institute, Washington.
Miller, D. ed. (1987), *The Blackwell Encyclopaedia of Political Thought*, Basil Blackwell Oxford
Rothbard, M. (1979), *Left and Right: The Prospects for Liberty*, Cato Institute, Washington.
Tucille, J. (1970), *Radical Libertarianism*, Bobbs-Merrill, New York

30) Against *Against Intellectual Property*: A Short Refutation of Meme Communism

(Libertarian Alliance online, 2015)

Introduction

This essay is intended to be a refutation of the main thesis in *Against Intellectual Property*, Kinsella 2008 (hereafter, K8). Points of agreement, relatively trivial disagreement, and irrelevant issues will largely be ignored, as will much repetition of errors in K8. Otherwise, the procedure is to go through K8 quoting various significantly erroneous parts as they arise and explaining the errors involved. It will not be necessary to respond at the same length as K8 itself.[1]

This text uses the new libertarian paradigm that is non-morally liberty-based, ultimately pre-propertarian, and critical-rationalist: that is, of liberty as the absence of interpersonal proactive impositions, of their minimisation in the event of clashes, and the explicitly conjectural nature of this theory and its desirability in practice.[2] This clashes with the old libertarian paradigm, which is mainly rights-based, ultimately (physical-) propertarian, and justificationist; as is found in the essay being criticised here.

The errors and their correction

K8 states that intellectual property (IP) rights "at least for patents and copyrights, may be considered rights in ideal objects"(14). And that seems to be clear enough. But then K8 goes on to assert that

> A's ownership of ideal rights gives him some degree of control—ownership—over the tangible property of innumerable others.(15)

This is a fundamental confusion. To own an "ideal object" (or abstraction, or meme) is to have control over its use. If someone tries to use that "ideal object" in some way (such as by making goods based on it) without its owner's consent, then a defence of its ownership may ensue. That defence is not asserting any kind of "ownership—over the tangible property of innumerable others." By analogy, if someone has ownership of his own body, or land, or any physical thing, then he might defend that ownership from other people using their own bodies or external properties to use it without his consent. And neither is that defence asserting any kind of "ownership—over the tangible property of innumerable others." Despite explicitly referring to "intellectual property", K8 is implicitly presupposing that only physical things can really be property and that any so-called IP is really about imposing limits on, or interfering with, 'real' physical property (PP).

However, there is a grain of truth in what K8 states, and it is this: to make anything into private property (whether physical, including self-ownership, or intellectual) is usually thereby to proactively impose at least very slightly on some other people: being denied free access can be a new disutility. But if we assume that such ownership is universalised, then those other people, in their turn, are also able to enjoy the benefits of private property. And in this way it is a lesser proactive imposition (i.e., a lesser interference with liberty) to allow (imposition-minimising) private property (whether physical or intellectual) than it is to deny it. Therefore, it is mistaken to view such private property (whether physical or intellectual) as "invasion" (36) or "trespass" (47) when it exists solely in order to minimise these things. K8 partly perceives and greatly magnifies the minimal imposition in IP but does not see any of the similar minimal imposition in PP. This is because K8 has adopted a purely physical-propertarian view as inherently 'libertarian' without having any explicit theory of liberty to explain this.

K8 immediately repeats this error but goes on to add more when it states that

> Patent and copyright invariably transfer partial ownership of tangible property from its natural owner to innovators, inventors, and artists.(15)

The idea of a "natural owner" is some sort of appeal to natural law. Perhaps natural law exists, and perhaps it is libertarian. But to cite it appears to be to adopt a natural law theory rather than an explicitly libertarian theory, i.e., a theory that explains the relationship to interpersonal liberty. Moreover, if there is a "natural owner" for some "tangible property" (by whatever explanation), then there ought also to be a "natural owner" for 'intangible property' (by a parallel explanation). And who must any "natural owner" be if not one of the "innovators, inventors, and artists" that produced it? Again, K8 is expressing a mere physical-propertarian presumption.

K8 goes on to assert that "Pro-IP arguments may be divided into natural-rights and utilitarian arguments" (16). What K8 overlooks here is that "Pro-IP arguments" can also include explicitly *libertarian* arguments: arguments that relate to liberty as such. And by asserting that "Libertarian IP advocates tend to adopt the former *justification*" (16, emphasis added) K8 is also overlooking the critical rationalist epistemology that can put IP as a libertarian conjecture for explanation and defence from criticism rather than any futile attempt at a "justification." This is because a putative justification implicitly and erroneously presupposes that it is possible to give epistemological support to a theory in a way that transcends a web of assumptions (or conjectural framework).[3] Hence, while there is no justification, it is still possible to conjecture and explain that there can be liberty-based IP, that it can promote 'utility' or general welfare (and libertarian 'natural rights' too), and then consider any criticisms that purport to show that it does not. But K8 is only arguing here that there are "fundamental problems with *justifying* any right or law on strictly utilitarian grounds" (20, emphasis added). As justifications are not possible, K8 is right, but not for the reasons it advances.

In the later discussion about "Property and Scarcity" K8 tells us that

> as libertarians recognize, following Locke, it is only the first occupier or user of such property that can be its natural owner. Only the *first-occupier* homesteading rule provides an objective, ethical, and non-arbitrary allocation of ownership in scarce resources.(30)

This, again, seems to be referring, without any theoretical explanation, to natural law in its reference to a "natural owner". So it seems to be about natural lawyers that merely, and mysteriously, self-identify as "libertarians". In fact, the "first occupier" rule does approximate to what is libertarian. But in order to see this one needs to have a theory of interpersonal liberty, such as 'not being proactively imposed on'. Then it follows that allowing the "first occupier" to have a property claim will slightly proactively impose on non-"first occupiers" who now have to go elsewhere (and might also be resentful, or envious, etc.). However, it would usually proactively impose more on people generally to not allow "first occupier" property claims: people would lose any investments they had made in the property and productive activity would be undermined. So "first occupier" ownership is proactive-imposition minimising (i.e., liberty maximising) as a strong ceteris paribus libertarian rule. But, in unusual or emergency situations, it is possible that "first occupier" ownership needs to be either completely waived or at least temporarily reduced. For instance, merely to be the first person to reach the sole natural water supply would not be enough to become its sole owner—as that would severely proactively impose on later-arriving people. And in the event of some natural disaster that meant that people needed to flee across other people's land, then a "first occupier" claim would not be enough to bar their way—as that would severely proactively impose on would-be escapees. This is because in both cases we have a pre-existing resource and not a benefit that the "first occupier" had created and was merely withholding access to. Thus this theory of liberty provides a better "objective, ethical, and non-arbitrary allocation of ownership in scarce resources." (Strictly speaking, of course, what the liberty-maximising option is remains a factual matter; while affirming that option's desirability is a, completely separate, moral or value matter.)

K8 continues:

> property rights ... are applicable only to scarce resources. Were we in a Garden of Eden where land and other goods were infinitely abundant, there would be no scarcity and, therefore, no need for property rules; property concepts would be meaningless. The idea of conflict, and the idea of rights, would not even arise.(31)

This cannot be entirely correct, if only because people would still want to own themselves (even if they were one of "infinitely abundant" clones). And there would probably also be value attached to particular examples of things ("This is the very locket she gave me on that day"). So it is not clear that "property concepts would be meaningless" just because "goods were infinitely abundant" in a physical sense. Such reservations aside, scarcity is a good explanation of the desirability of property rules: those rules can maximise liberty (by minimising proactive impositions) with all the advantages of so doing.

However, it is another fundamental error to go on to assert that "The problem with IP rights is that the ideal objects protected by IP rights are not scarce" (31). This is an error because each ideal object is a particular thing. There is only one ideal object that is Pythagoras's Theorem, the number six, and Mahler's second symphony (which is not to imply that all these should be IP). And there is a finite supply of *valuable* "ideal objects" that currently exist; often with no close substitute for a particular one. K8 is not taking the theory of "ideal objects" seriously as particular "objects". Infinitely more than one physical use or physical instantiation of an ideal object might be possible. But that does not show that there is more than one ideal object of that kind. It makes sense to say that there is an ideal object that is a particular poem. But there cannot be two or more ideal objects that are this same poem. They conceptually collapse into the same one ideal object. What K8 really means, of course, is simply that the physical use of an ideal object does not deprive other people of that ideal object's use in any way. But that is false as well, because one very important use for an ideal object just is to own it, and that ownership implies that the owner has control over its use.[4] K8 is advocating the non-ownership (or communism) of ideal objects. But that non-ownership will cause a 'tragedy of the commons' as regards many ideal objects: people will be less likely to attempt to produce (including by discovery) some ideal objects if they cannot own (exclusively control) them once they are produced.

Consider a physical analogy. Suppose I build a machine that can produce widgets using air and natural light. The machine is also powered by air and natural light and never needs repairing. I switch on the machine and in seconds I have a month's supply of widgets to sell in the nearby market. When I am not around, you come along and use the machine to make the same number of widgets and you promptly go and sell them in the market yourself. Furthermore, you intend to continue repeating the procedure because I am, somehow, unable to guard the machine adequately and you can always, somehow, beat me to the market. You assert that I have lost nothing, because I still have access to my machine, and to the widgets I made, and to as many more widgets as I want. However, I didn't produce the machine or the widgets for my personal use. I produced them solely in order to have something to sell. And now you have prevented that. Therefore, it is clearly false to claim that I have lost nothing and that my incentive to make such machines has not been undermined. And this appears to be sufficiently analogous with the position of many people who produce "ideal objects" with the intention of claiming them as IP. Perhaps this is generally fairly obvious and convincing to most people who consider such matters. Confusion mainly arises if we allow the crude and false, and 'mutually reinforcing', assumptions that only physical things can really be property, that there is no scarcity involved with valuable ideas, and that both any alleged IP "justice" (20) or consequentialist need to "encourage the production of creative works and inventions" (21) must to be "justified" (passim)—which must not, in any case, constrain 'real' PP.

K8 then makes a further error in asserting that "such property rights are not, and cannot be, allocated in accordance with the first occupier homesteading rule" (31-32). In fact, the first inventor or discoverer of an intellectual object could be regarded as a "first occupier homesteading" it. The only problem would be the even greater crudeness of that rule in this case. For, in order to avoid being a positive nuisance to (i.e., proactively imposing on) other people, it is necessary to time-limit the (sole) ownership to likely (or actual) independent invention or discovery. Some sort of legal procedure involving experts would probably be required to approximate the non-proactively-imposing length of a claim, and any claims would likely always be liable to later appeals. Any real second party, etc., would then share the IP. Otherwise, it would eventually revert to the public domain once there were only hypothetical further parties.

One example K8 then gives us is this:

> If I invent a technique for harvesting cotton, your harvesting cotton in this way would not take away the technique from me. I still have my technique (as well as my cotton). Your use does not exclude my use; we could both use my technique to harvest cotton. There is no economic scarcity, and no possibility of conflict over the use of a scarce resource. Thus, there is no need for exclusivity.(32)

Bearing in mind what has now been explained—and taking the possibility of IP seriously—this can more accurately and relevantly be reworded thus: If I invent a technique for harvesting cotton [intending to own that technique], your harvesting cotton in this way [without my consent] would [~~not~~] take away the [ownership of the] technique from me. I [do not] still have my [IP] technique (as well as my cotton). Your [non-contractual] use does [~~not~~] exclude my [IP] use; we could both use my technique to harvest cotton [but I have lost the IP in the technique]. There is [~~no~~] economic scarcity [in both the ownership and in the general supply of useful ideal objects], and [~~no~~ thereby a] possibility of conflict over the use of a scarce resource. Thus, there is [~~no~~] need for [IP] exclusivity.

Or consider this remark in K8:

> Ideas are not naturally scarce. However, by recognizing a right in an ideal object, one creates scarcity where none existed before. (33)

As we have seen, there is both a "natural" scarcity of valuable ideas generally and also a scarcity with a particular idea in that a denial of (proactive-imposition-minimising) producer-ownership does deprive the producer of the intellectual asset he has created, and thereby a considerable part of the incentive to produce valuable ideas. Hence to deny such producer-ownership is to exacerbate scarcity (in opportunity cost terms) among valuable ideas. Of course, in the very short term the abolition of IP would in some sense reduce scarcity. But this is relevantly and sufficiently similar to the way that a reduction in scarcity would occur if factories, warehouses, and shops were denied ownership of their physical products: any immediate increase in supply would very soon turn into greater scarcity than would otherwise have existed.

It is unnecessary to continue further with K8. The remainder of the text contains more repetition, plus quotations from texts expressing similar views, or material that is irrelevant to the main argument.

Conclusion

In its advocacy of "ideal object" (or meme) communism, K8 makes various significant errors throughout. The two main errors are assuming that only physical things can really be property, and that there is no scarcity involved with ideal objects. Many of the errors might have been avoided if only K8 had an explicit, non-moral, theory of interpersonal liberty by which to assess what is libertarian. In other words, K8 would not have had to resort to the old gallimaufry of dubious ad hoc assumptions presented as "libertarianism" if only it had taken liberty more seriously—as the new libertarian paradigm does.

Notes

[1] A general explanation of the position taken here is explained in Lester [2000] 2012, pp. 95-105. A concise but in some ways more precise and detailed explanation is in the entry on intellectual property in Lester Forthcoming and online here: http://thelibertarianalliance.com/2014/09/06/thoughts-on-intellectual-property/
[2] As found, for instance, in Lester [2000] 2012, 2011, 2014, and Forthcoming. The exact form of words does not matter, but it must be possible to express interpersonal liberty (in the intuitive sense of 'people not initiating constraints on each other') in some adequate form of words, as the old paradigm fails to do. The formula chosen here is intended to reflect the idea that the relevant constraints must be somehow initiated (rather than defensive or neutral) and must lower the want-satisfaction (or preference utility) of the recipient.
[3] For further explanation of critical rationalism and its application to libertarianism see, for instance, Lester 2011 ch. 23; Lester [2000] 2012 pp.135-142; Lester 2014 pp. 74-76 and 107-109; and relevant entries in Lester Forthcoming.
[4] Even if we suppose that ideal objects are somehow multiple, that multiple supply is still scarce in the sense that there are limited ownership rights of that supply: either particular people own it or it is not owned at all.

Bibliography

Kinsella, N. Stephan. 2008. *Against Intellectual Property*. Auburn, Alabama: Ludwig von Mises Institute.
Lester, J. C. 2011. *Arguments for Liberty: a Libertarian Miscellany*. Buckingham: The University of Buckingham Press.
——. [2000] 2012. *Escape from Leviathan: Libertarianism without Justificationism*. Buckingham: The University of Buckingham Press.
——. 2014. *Explaining Libertarianism: Some Philosophical Arguments*. Buckingham: The University of Buckingham Press.
——. Forthcoming. *A Libertarian Dictionary: Explaining a Libertarian Theory*.

31) A response[1] to "Libertarianism and pollution: the limits of absolutist moralism"[2]

(Libertarian Alliance online, 2015)

We are first told that

> Some of the currently most popular forms of libertarian thought are defined by a commitment to the "non-aggression principle" – a principle which holds that it is always wrong to initiate physical force against other human beings.

Although "popular", this is a poor expression of libertarianism. "Aggression" is problematic as being what libertarians are against. For one thing, it is rarely explained exactly how non-aggression is supposed to relate to a theory of interpersonal liberty. For another, "non-aggression", in plain English, is no more up to the task than "non-coercion" (another libertarian favourite, although less popular of late)—not without charitable interpretation, at least. As glossed in the above quotation, "aggression" clearly does not work for two main reasons. 1) Theft and fraud don't need to involve anyone having to "initiate physical force against other human beings": you don't need to initiate physical force against me in order to steal my money or cheat me out of it. 2) Consequently, it will sometimes be necessary to "initiate physical force" against thieves and fraudsters: to arrest them and bring them to trial, for instance.

That said, we can try to make a little more sense of the "non-aggression principle" (NAP); partly because many libertarians use it, and partly in order to move towards something clearer. Therefore, we might, as above suggested, provide a charitable interpretation of "aggression", e.g., 'the proactive interference with the bodies and external property of other people (where that property is itself not acquired by proactive interference)'. And if we do that, then it begins to make sense that the absence of such "aggression" is what interpersonal liberty is (although this sets aside various precise philosophical problems with this account). For such "aggression" against us would be other people initiating constraints on us. And we can then make sense of interpersonal liberty as the absence of such initiated constraints. (However, it ought at least to be mentioned that what liberty is—as a theory and as social phenomena—is a factual matter that is completely separate from the moral issue of whether breaching such liberty is "always wrong". Conflating the two issues, as the article does, is a major source of confusion.)

Having rectified that account of the "non-aggression principle" sufficiently for our current purposes, we can now proceed to the second major error in the article:

> The problem is that libertarianism seems to imply that environmental pollution, insofar as it constitutes or involves aggression against other human beings, is morally impermissible. Not just a bad thing, mind you, but absolutely morally impermissible in the same way that theft, assault, and murder are.

The error here is easily explained. The "non-aggression principle"—as interpreted here, at least—is best seen as being what observing liberty fully or absolutely would require. That is, full liberty is the absence of any "aggression" (i.e, proactive interference with people and their—non-proactively interfering—property). Now, it is true that pollution will be "aggressive" in this sense. But that is only half of the story. Because to prohibit the activities that are causing the pollution will also be "aggressive". Consider a simple example. If I have a fire for warmth and cooking, then you might suffer some minor pollution as a result. But if you can force me not to have a fire, then you have deprived me of warmth and cooking. Both the allowance and the prohibition of pollution will be "aggressions" (although 'proactive impositions' seems to be a clearer expression). Whichever one is preferred, or however they are balanced, there will be some "aggression". Therefore, it is impossible to implement the non-aggression principle in the event of such clashes. So what is the libertarian solution? It is surely libertarian to maximise liberty as far as is practical. That means adopting a minimum-aggression principle (or MAP). And that probably involves compromise and possibly compensation. How are minimum aggressions to be determined? They can often best be measured, traded, and compensated for by assigning market—or, at least, reasonable—monetary values to the gains and losses involved. In any event, the general solution to the problem is to see the NAP as referring to observing liberty when matters are one-sided. But the MAP applies when there are clashes.

Note that this proffered solution is not, as the article suggests, restricted to "discrete interactions between identifiable individuals". It applies just as much to "a world increasingly characterised by the complexly interrelated activities of large numbers of dispersed individuals". But to engage in, say, class actions (as the legal term has it) over "contemporary environmental problems such as automobile pollution, acid rain, and global climate change" is not in any anti-libertarian sense to be "less individualistic in identifying perpetrators and victims". However, there is an important equivocation here. In one sense, rules that are intended to protect the general public (rather than any individuals in particular) are thereby, ipso facto, not "individualistic". But they can remain individualistic in the libertarian sense that is opposed to collectivism (whereby individuals cease to have claims to liberty because of the greater good of the majority). Such individualism-in-principle is not abandoned just because there are lot of indeterminate people involved. Neither is the MAP in principle "less absolutist". This is because liberty remains the thing that must absolutely be maximised. Consequently, it is clearly possible to "*keep* the individualism and absolutism where it makes sense" because, as interpreted here, it makes sense everywhere.

Then we are asked this question:

> How can libertarians still maintain that it is wrong to impose a small tax on the wealthy, even if the social benefits would be enormous, while allowing that drivers are entitled to send small amounts of toxins into other people's lungs since, after all, the social benefits of driving are enormous?

The question is confused in two main ways. First, no libertarian need concede that it is even practical "to impose a small tax on the wealthy" such that "the social benefits would be enormous". This mere logical possibility flies in the face of the deleterious unintended consequences of tax-transfers. In an imaginary world, the state might be a welfare boon. In reality, it is a welfare bane. There is no sound reason to suppose that "utilitarianism" must in practice "countenance violations of individual rights". Second, it is, at best, a muddle to describe the libertarian case for allowing the "toxins" caused by driving as being because "the social benefits are enormous". It is, again, necessary to look at both sides before applying the MAP. 1) Allowing driving despite its toxins: this will proactively impose ("aggress") to a minuscule degree on people (probably too small to make compensation claims economic in most cases); and this has to include a deduction to the extent that any particular individuals also engage in driving, or benefit from the consequences of driving (such as the delivery of goods to their area, etc.), or chose to move into an area where driving is allowed, etc. 2) Banning driving because of its toxins: this would proactively impose huge costs, in one way or another, on almost everyone. Hence, 1 is the liberty-maximising option.

If the foregoing analysis is roughly correct, then the answer is not "waiting to be discovered by future libertarian philosophers".[3] And it is more mere fantasy and confusion to suppose that any solution must ultimately mean "pushing libertarians back ... toward the more moderate classical liberalism of Adam Smith, David Hume, and Friedrich Hayek".

Clarificatory conclusion

Because of the way that the problem was originally framed, it is easy to misinterpret the above response. In particular, it might look as though it amounts to a moral advocacy of a sort of consequentialist libertarianism to replace deontological libertarianism. It does not. And such an interpretation would be to miss the crucial main point in a typical way. For the response is not really about libertarian morals. It is about what interpersonal liberty is (in abstract theory) and what applying it objectively entails (in normal practice). Most self-identified libertarians unwittingly have a moral muddle without a central factual theory of liberty. They cannot yet see that they first need to sort out what liberty is, and therefore entails if instantiated, and only after that can moral questions about it be coherently raised and tackled. An analogical error would be utilitarians who could not even give an account of utility.

Notes

[1] The article in question repeats a criticism of libertarianism that was one of those raised (http://www.libertarianism.org/blog/libertarianism-pollution) and briefly answered (http://www.libertarianism.org/blog/pollution-minimizing-aggression) on libertarianism.org. The revised replies to those criticisms are now available in a book chapter (Lester 2014, Ch. 5). But as the new article is somewhat different, and the audience different, a reconsideration of these important issues seems merited.
[2] IEA Blog, 20 February 2015: http://www.iea.org.uk/blog/libertarianism-and-pollution-the-limits-of-absolutist-moralism
[3] It ought to be noted that any attempt to refute this overall theoretical approach that is based on criticisms in Gordon and Modugno 2003 or Frederick 2013, ought at least to be aware of the replies to those criticisms: chapters 9 and 10 in Lester 2014.

Bibliography

Gordon, David and Modugno, Roberta A. 2003. "Review of J.C. Lester's *Escape from Leviathan: Liberty, Welfare, and Anarchy Reconciled*." *Journal of Libertarian Studies* 17, 4: 101–109.
Frederick, Danny. 2013. "A Critique of Lester's Account of Liberty." *Libertarian Papers* 5, 1: 45-66. Online here: http://libertarianpapers.org/article/2-frederick-critique-of-lesters-account/
Lester, J. C. 2011. *Arguments for Liberty: a Libertarian Miscellany*. Buckingham: The University of Buckingham Press.

——. [2000] 2012. *Escape from Leviathan: Libertarianism Without Justificationism*. Buckingham: The University of Buckingham Press.
——. 2014. *Explaining Libertarianism: Some Philosophical Arguments*. Buckingham: The University of Buckingham Press.
Zwolinski, Matt. 2015. "Libertarianism and pollution: the limits of absolutist moralism", Institute of Economic Affairs, Blog, 20 February. Online here: http://www.iea.org.uk/blog/libertarianism-and-pollution-the-limits-of-absolutist-moralism

32) IP, the NAP, and Pre-Propertarian Liberty: New-Paradigm Libertarian Replies to some Rothbardian Criticisms

The context

Andy Curzon replied (often quoting from the opening sections of Lester 2014, chapter 10) in an on-going debate with Lee Waaks, which Mr Waaks forwarded (with approval) to the Libertarian Alliance Forum (27 February 2015). This response replies to the criticisms after directly quoting them (the indented text; except where Lester is occasionally quoted, as indicated). A few cuts have been made to avoid some repetition and irrelevance. However, just as Mr Curzon sometimes repeats his main points in slightly different ways and contexts in the hope that some of them might prove cogent, so this reply does the same. The dialogue-like result seems to engage more directly and completely than producing a new stand-alone exposition. And some new arguments are even developed in the process. But the full nature of many of the criticisms and replies often only becomes clear as the "dialogue" proceeds. An addendum then rebuts two further brief critical responses in the same manner.

Criticisms and replies

> ... there is no more to say because you keep replying words to the effect of this quote from your sent reply
> --- 'Good ideas are scarce (i.e. limited) because if they were not, they would already exist.' ---

The word 'idea' is ambiguous and too suggestive of a link to minds. Hence it seems preferable to adopt 'meme' to help mnemonicise Karl Popper's three worlds (ontological categories) theory. World 1, Matter: all that is physical. World 2, Minds: all that is conscious. World 3, Memes: all materially encoded abstractions. To which, therefore, it seems necessary to add (as Popper appears not to have clearly seen, but David McDonagh has[1]) an immaterial and atemporal World 0, here called Modes: all abstractions. Not all memes are (or have been, or will ever be) 'ideas' in any mind. A book of computer-generated logarithms, or poetry, or patterns, etc., might contain materially encoded abstractions that have never been consciously perceived. Only an infinitely small fraction of W0 modes will ever be instantiated in W1 matter, or perceived in W2 minds, or recorded in W3 memes.

Scarcity relates to memes in, at least, these ways:

1) The number of (useful) memes is scarce (not infinite).
2) Each meme is about only one mode (abstraction or 'intellectual object').
3) Ownership (right of use and control) of any particular meme is itself scarce (like ownership of a particular piece of matter, such as land).
4) The production (via discovery, invention, or creation) of a meme requires the use of scarce resources (even if mainly thought and time).

> That is missing the point of why scarcity is important [l]inked in with physical boundaries. Of course ideas are not limited, if the[y] are then SHOW ME THEIR LIMITS! Show me the limits of one single good idea.

The same meme (materially-encoded mode) might be expressed in many physical ways—each of them physically limited, of course. But the mode itself that the meme captures is an abstraction, and so does not have "physical boundaries"; it has abstract boundaries. Pythagoras's theorem is not Pi, and it is easy to distinguish them.

> ...think about applying this to anything. It is ridiculous...the whole point of practical scarcity is that it DOES APPLY TO THINGS THAT EXIST.

Particular memes are often known (i.e., grasped by minds) to exist. Unknown modes are not (yet) known to exist but they already have abstract existence and objective qualities (such as a number that has never yet been thought of or written down but which is entailed by the existence of numbers). "Good ideas" are known useful memes. Scarcity relates to them in the senses already outlined. But they are collectively less scarce thanks to the incentive effects of intellectual property (IP)—although some people do not require that incentive, of course.

> So I hear your song that you have 'IP protected' and then want to play it on my guitar but am estopped from this in law! What right does anyone have to stop me plucking whatever strings I choose to so long as it is my guitar?

They have a right because you thereby make use of someone else's property, namely their intellectual property (although some personal uses are often not a practical concern). One may not use one's property (of whatever type) to trespass on other people's property (of whatever type). It's not possible to refute intellectual property by simply presupposing that only physical property is 'real' property.

> Liberty as in the 'NAP' (i.e. if the NAP is not broken in any way one has 'liberty', or 'autonomy')…

How does the NAP (non-aggression principle) relate to interpersonal liberty or autonomy? It doesn't mention either.

> …can only apply to physical goods because when I see/hear/use your idea you have not lost out

If the producers' *claimed* ownership of intellectual products is not observed, then that is an immediate loss to the would-be owners (or they wouldn't be "would-be owners"). Very soon, such uncivilised meme communism is a loss to everyone.

> Imagine a world from 1,000 years ago where everyone's ideas were 'protected'! We would be centuries behind where we are now…innovation would be stifled!

This overlooks, or fails to grasp, 1) the new-paradigm's proactive-imposition limit to intellectual-property duration: probable or actual independent production,[2] and 2) the incentive effect of allowing such IP.

> Lester thinks 'we must have a theory of liberty before a theory of property'

There are infinite possible property rules. Some property rules fit interpersonal liberty and most do not. Only a separate theory of liberty can distinguish the two categories. The basic libertarian conception of interpersonal liberty does not need to mention property: it is about people not being proactively constrained by each other (more than is unavoidable, at least).

> but 'liberty' is a negative concept, not a positive concept, as agreed by both Lester and anti-IP people.

It seems as though a "negative concept" can often be reworded into a "positive concept", so this does not appear to be a very substantive point.

> One can not have liberty TO DO everything, otherwise that would extend to hurting other people and such.

In the Lockean sense, one can "have liberty TO DO everything" within one's abilities, resources, etc. Proactively "hurting other people" is *licence* or power rather than liberty.

> So what I mean by negative is that it is the freedom not to infringe on anyone else's liberty.

That is an obscure sentence. Is it supposed to explain "negative" freedom? Or "negative" liberty? In one sense, everyone has the "freedom not to infringe on anyone else's liberty"—but they sometimes do it anyway. In any case, freedom and liberty are synonyms in English and so they cannot usefully be contrasted or used to explain each other (if that is what is intended) except by stipulating a difference (e.g., Hobbesian physical freedom versus Lockean interpersonal, or social, liberty).

> I have read everything Lester writes on this (I think)

Including the three books?

> and he goes round in circles

Rothbardian (and Nozickian) libertarianism circles around various key ideas without ever clearly relating them to interpersonal liberty. By contrast, the new-paradigm libertarianism ultimately relates everything back to a theory of liberty.

> So 'libertarianism', as far as the modern conception is concerned is the 'NAP' or 'consent axiom' (if both people consent to a physical act then it is legal).

This does not explain how interpersonal liberty, as such, relates to either the 'NAP' or the 'consent axiom'. Abstractly theorised, interpersonal liberty can be interpreted as the absence of people's proactive constraints on each other's chosen goals (or preference-satisfactions). This abstract interpretation does not mention property or law. For it is a contingent matter whether property, and if so which forms, will best fit it. In the world we live in, it does indeed appear that self-ownership, (proactive-constraint-minimising) private property, voluntary transfers, consensual activities, contracts, etc., facilitate such liberty. But, in order to be philosophically clear, the contingent nature of these various practical connections needs to be acknowledged and explained.

> Here I go back to the fact that no-one is losing out once an idea has been created […] and as such it is not 'aggressive' for me to adapt your idea since you can still use the idea whether I do so or not. I really don't see how this can be logically ignored.

Here is a relevant reply (now also in chapter 30, p.151) which is itself being ignored or overlooked:

Consider a physical analogy. Suppose I build a machine that can produce widgets using air and natural light. The machine is also powered by air and natural light and never needs repairing. I switch on the machine and in seconds I have a month's supply of widgets to sell in the nearby market. When I am not around, you come along and use the machine to make the same number of widgets and you promptly go and sell them in the market yourself. Furthermore, you intend to continue repeating the procedure because I am, somehow, unable to guard the machine adequately and you can always, somehow, beat me to the market. You assert that I have lost nothing, because I still have access to my machine, and to the widgets I made, and to as many more widgets as I want. However, I didn't produce the machine or the widgets for my personal use. I produced them solely in order to have something to sell. And now you have prevented that. Therefore, it is clearly false to claim that I have lost nothing and that my incentive to make such machines has not been undermined. And this appears to be sufficiently analogous with the position of many people who produce "ideal objects" with the intention of claiming them as IP.

Back to the criticisms:

> So when you say [...]
> --- [...] libertarians attempt to justify property rights by various arguments but they don't have an explicit theory of liberty' ---
> this is hogwash since libertarians' theory of liberty is precisely the freedom to use one's body and property as one chooses. THAT IS THE LIBERTY THEY EXPLAIN.

So "liberty" is supposed to be "the freedom to use one's body and property as one chooses". As already mentioned, "liberty" and "freedom" are synonyms, so the latter cannot be used to explain the former. And this does not explain exactly how "to use one's body and property as one chooses" is interpersonal liberty in itself. It looks far more like what usually fits *theoretical* liberty in *practice*. Theoretical liberty itself is, more like, the absence of interpersonal proactive constraints. Moreover, the offered "libertarians' theory of liberty" is silent on which of the infinite possible property rules are meant (presumably, only the ones that fit liberty; but we are given no theoretical criterion for this). Therefore, there is no proper "libertarians' theory of liberty" here; "It isn't even wrong" (as Wolfgang Pauli used to hyperbolise about confused theories in physics). It conflates the practical and the theoretical by tacitly relying on intuitions about what is meant. It is the equivalent of a socialist purporting to give a theory of human 'liberty' in itself as 'free access to the goods one needs'.

> When he writes
> --- 'How are the different kinds of property being distinguished as libertarian or not libertarian?' ---
> no-one claims property itself as libertarian - that would be absurd!

Some types of property are usually libertarian in practice and some are not. Only a pre-propertarian theory of liberty can distinguish them.

> Libertarian is from the word liberty which means freedom.

'Liberty' means 'freedom' and vice versa. But what is interpersonal liberty or freedom?

> So, when Lester says
> --- 'But libertarians usually have no explicit theory of what such liberty is. So they must have a tacit theory of liberty' ---
> he is plain wrong. The explicit theory of liberty is as stated: 'The allowance to use one's property (including one's own body) as far as one chooses, so long as it does not infringe on someone else's property'.

Three responses:
1) That so-called "explicit theory of liberty" is an interpretation of liberty in practice. There is no explanation relating this practice to a genuine theory, or concept, or even definition of interpersonal liberty in itself.
2) This does not explain which kind(s) of "one's property" (out of infinite possibilities) this applies to. Presumably, only property that fits interpersonal liberty. But which is that? Without a pre-propertarian theory of liberty we cannot say.
3) As it stands, any kind of statist might agree with the account given. For instance, they might (and often do) say that once 'legitimate' taxation is due then one simply ceases to own that money.

> Once again, as explained, of course one can not talk of liberty without talking of one's own body (property) or the other way round

Four responses:
1) Abstractly theorised, interpersonal liberty is people not proactively constraining each other. This would still be true if we were, somehow, minds without bodies.
2) Of course, we do have bodies. But one's body is not inherently "property" (as a legal institution); in a 'state of nature', for instance.
3) It is always a separate question whether, and which, and how, certain kinds of property fit interpersonal liberty.
4) As to "the other way round": clearly one can also talk of "one's own body" without talking of liberty or even implying anything about it (e.g., "My body is the phenotypical expression of particular genes").

> Liberty and property are INEXTRICABLY linked.

Property is possible without (much) interpersonal liberty: in a totalitarian system for instance. And liberty is possible without any property: if a group of people were to live together without property but without interfering with each other or the things people are using, then they would all have (maximal) liberty.

> There is no need for a 'tacit theory of liberty' when one has an explicit theory of it.

Quite right. But the alleged "explicit theory" is not even a real theory of liberty.

> Imagine if you signed a contract and then someone challenged something you did that was not prohibited by the contract and claimed this to be 'tacit'!

In fact, contracts often (always?) have tacit or implied aspects. Sometimes a court case is required to determine what these are.

> This is why contract[s] are so good, and can be applied even to [i]ntellectual endeavours.

It is difficult to impossible to write an exhaustive and completely unambiguous contract. Language is broad and relies on shared tacit understanding. But basic property (whether physical or intellectual) is not based on contract theory.

> Now this is important [...] - something you may not have considered yet: One of the reasons I am against 'IP', as well as it making no sense, is that in law it is pointless. And it is pointless (or better 'superfluous') precisely because of EXPLICIT contracts. Now if I write a book and make people who buy them explicitly sign a contract not to use more than, say '100 words in a row from anywhere in the book in the publishing of any other writing', or something similar, then it is their choice, BEFORE THEY BUY OR READ THE BOOK (in the case of a book) and as such if they re-publish 100 words or more they are breaking EXPLICIT parts of the contract. Do you see? So what is the need for 'IP law' given this? There is none.

This does not deal with people who are not party to the contract: someone who finds a lost book, or overhears its being read, or photographs a page over someone's shoulder, etc. One might as well say that physical property can be based on contracts alone. It would be necessary, but completely impracticable, to have contracts with everyone—including future generations. As economists would say, transactions costs would be prohibitive.

> The same can be applied to inventions or anything of an intellectual creation.

And the same answer applies.

> So I make a new toy for children that I think is going to be 'big'. If I want to protect this properly, and as far as is fair (i.e. I don't own the money from selling my products until people have actually bought the product, so I can not lay claim to money I have not yet received), then it is up to me to write a contract for people to sign. This can even go so far as stipulating, EXPLICITLY, that this toy must not be copied within certain bounds by the buyer. But clearly this can not extend to people who have not signed the contract - that would be ridiculous. OK I think this is clear now.

Clear and clearly impractical. Any non-buyer who sees the toy can copy it.

> Continuing on with Lester's quote, when he writes
> --- 'Otherwise, we could not explain why one kind of property is compatible with liberty while another kind is not' ---
> he is going down a stupid path because all 'property' (physical things that one can logically and practically own) IS within the remit of liberty.

It is philosophically naive to conflate liberty and property. And the mainstream libertarian position conflates liberty, property, and morals. But this is hidden by a delusion of being completely clear and simple.

> if an idea can be copied, so long as there has been no theft of the idea, or fraud etc, then THE CREATOR DOES NOT LOSE THE USE OF THIS INTELLECTUAL IDEA.

He loses the use of it as property, which is often the main or even sole reason for his creating or discovering it in the first place.

> ... when Lester puts
> --- 'it looks as though there must be a tacit theory of pre-propertarian liberty' ---
> of course there need be no TACIT theory when we have a perfectly good EXPLICIT theory of liberty (NAP).

The NAP does not give an explicit explanation of interpersonal liberty; it doesn't even mention liberty.

> This (something explicit) has the obvious added benefit of being clear and objective, whereas things that are 'tacit' have not been agreed upon explicitly, by definition.

The tacit theory that mainstream libertarianism presupposes has now been made explicit in the new paradigm. The truth of that explicit theory has nothing to do with anyone's agreement with it.

> That sounds like a word-play but it is not. Really think about it. This is what is called the 'Hobbesian Myth'...i.e. - by living under the remit of a monopoly state we 'tacitly' agree to do whatever we are told by the monopoly state, under every circumstance. But no-one had agreed to this explicitly so how can it be so?!!!!

The falsity of Hobbes's tacit *political* contract theory is irrelevant to the assertion that mainstream libertarianism entails a tacit theory of liberty-in-itself that can be made explicit. In any case, there is a true tacit *social* contract theory: that people should associate without proactively imposing on each other. That is why people usually interact without fear and suspicion.

> I need not point out the illogicality behind this statement
> --- 'And if there is such a tacit theory, then it ought to be possible—and should be enlightening—to make this tacit theory explicit' ---
> other than to just quote it. There is no sense to this. I have nothing to say on this other than it is ludicrous and like me calling an apple a pear or a square a duck. What is the point? Tacit is tacit and explicit is explicit.

Some things are tacit. And what is tacit can often be made explicit. This is not any kind of "illogicality". One might as well say that what is hidden cannot be revealed, because 'hidden is hidden and revealed is revealed'.

> the key is ACTUAL EXPLICIT AGREEMENT by both sides, of course...the consent axiom again.

The key to what? A real theory of liberty? How?

> Is this arbitrary, no! Otherwise, again, it could be claimed you 'tacitly' agreed to an[y] number of things under the sun.

It could. And some of them would be true and others false. People do tacitly agree to things. To go into a restaurant and order food (perhaps without even looking at the menu) is tacitly to agree to pay for it afterwards. The waiter never bothers to point this out. To offer something for sale, is tacitly to imply that it is yours to sell and fit for its apparent purpose. And so on.

> For me, the heart of Lester's inanity lies here

> --- '[…] they write about being against (initiated) coercion or aggression as the implied opposite of liberty, without explaining exactly how these are theoretically related to liberty.' ---
> There is no problem explicitly explaining the NAP at all. If there is one he should explain the problem.

It is explained. It ought to be clear enough, but let's try again. The *cited problem* is relating the allegedly "libertarian" NAP to liberty itself. The NAP holds that certain property rights are legitimate and then defines 'aggression' as the flouting of those property rights. At no point does the NAP even mention liberty, let alone explain how this account relates to liberty.

> It is a negative rule - to have interpersonal liberty (liberty with more than one person on[] the planet)

This does not explain what liberty is.

> one must put bounds on the ability to do what one wishes BECAUSE THINGS THAT EXIST ARE SCARCE.

This is often true. But how does this relate to liberty?

> Circles circles circles.

As explained, the irony here is that it is Rothbardism that tries to explain itself by circling around non-aggression, explicit consent, legitimate property, self-ownership, scarcity, homesteading, etc., without at any time providing an explicit theory of interpersonal liberty or how these things relate to it. They do relate to liberty, but it is left tacit or unexplained. This is like a utilitarian explaining consequentialism, the importance of maximising utility, the difference between act and rule utilitarianism, average versus total utility, and so on, without at any time explaining explicitly what *utility*, in itself, is. But utilitarians don't usually do this. They usually tell you what theory of utility they are using (whether some kind of happiness, or pleasure, or preference-satisfaction, etc.). There is an embarrassing hole at the heart of mainstream libertarianism: there is no explicit theory of interpersonal liberty in itself.

> Liberty is freedom to do what one wishes..this is the base theory of liberty which I think no-one disagrees with.

There are two main theories of liberty in modern political philosophy. The egoistic, and materialistic, Hobbesian one is the absence of any constraints on a person. It is, roughly, the "freedom to do what one wishes". And that is, more or less, a zero-sum theory by which liberties conflict and one person's gain in liberty is often another's loss (but, strictly, Hobbes does not restrict it to other people as constraints). On this account, a slave-owner has more liberty at the expense of his slave's liberty. However, that is not "the base theory of liberty which ... no-one disagrees with." For there is also the social, or interpersonal, Lockean theory of liberty. That is, roughly, about people not being *proactively* constrained by each other. And in this sense people's liberties are not at each other's expense. For the slave-owner has proactive power over the slave, but no extra liberty thereby. Only some version of this Lockean sense of liberty is properly the libertarian one (although there are some Hobbesian libertarians, as we shall see).

> But because resources and land and space are scarce, we caveat this with 'so long as it does not infringe on other people's property'.

Logically, there is no end of possible property rules. Under some of them chattel slavery is allowed. Hence the slave would be infringing on his master's property by running away. Therefore, the expression "so long as it does not infringe on other people's property" is tacitly assuming that such property is in accord with liberty—in some libertarian sense—rather than flouting it. But we have been offered no independent theory of liberty by which to judge this. There is only the circling around of the various mainstream concepts of self-ownership, homesteading, voluntarism, scarcity, etc.

> His next paragraph on coercion is just irrelevant, if not a mild straw-man. No-one (I have heard of anyway) claims infringement on liberty is based on coercion.

Here is a handful of examples of some relatively well-known people using "coercion" to explain liberty (or freedom). This is not to imply that they always or only explain liberty in this way. In *The Ethics of Liberty*, here is Murray Rothbard approving of Hayek's definition of freedom:

> ... F.A. Hayek attempts to establish a systematic political philosophy on behalf of individual liberty. He begins very well, by defining freedom as the absence of coercion... (219)

In *Capitalism: The Unknown Ideal*, Ayn Rand writes,

> ...freedom, in a political context, has only one meaning: *the absence of physical coercion*. (Ch.3, 43; emphasis in the original)

In his *Capitalism and Freedom: Fortieth Anniversary Edition*, Milton Friedman asserts that

> Political freedom means the absence of coercion of a man by his fellow man. (15)

In *The Philosophic Thought of Ayn Rand,* Douglas J. Den Uyl and Douglas B. Rasmussen say,

> …liberty is by definition an absence of coercion… (212)

In *Classical Individualism: The Supreme Importance of Each Human Being,* Tibor Machan also says:

> …liberty is by definition an absence of coercion… (184).

And if this use of "coercion" does not (or did not) happen relatively often with many libertarians, then why was this complaint made, on his blog, by Stephan Kinsella?:

> I must confess that one of my nits is the use by libertarians of the word "coercion" to mean "aggression."
> (http://www.stephankinsella.com/2009/08/the-problem-with-coercion/)

Not that "aggression" is much clearer of course; not without a very charitable interpretation and a proper theory of liberty.

The criticisms continue:

> He then tries to use this straw-man to talk of defense. Well defense is another matter.

As we have seen, it is not a straw man. And it is not "another matter" given that the relationship between coercion and defence is being discussed.

> Of course if you steal from me and then you are punished this technically infringes on your property, but this is what we have the law for!

If someone steals, then it is not necessary within libertarian theory that he be "punished". He needs to pay full restitution, assuming the victim or his assigns require it. However, that can include a risk-multiplier (relating to the chance of evading detection). And some of it might be taken in the form of retributive restitution. This is now covered in this book (Lester 2015, chapter 27) and Lester 2012 (chapter 3, 108-120). Neither does this entail that this "infringes on your property". Because if restitution is due from someone, then it is not infringing on his property to take it: that property has been forfeit. It might well be that many such matters would be dealt with via libertarian law. But it should be noted that observing liberty objectively entails such restitution prior to any legal system or even property itself. All such precise philosophical distinctions are lost within the crude, conflationist, cult of mainstream libertarianism.

> I am not claiming to have an exact position on the exact punishment for every aggressive action, neither is anybody theoretically,

In fact, the theory of restitution in the cited chapters of Lester do, in principle, claim "to have an exact position on the exact [restitution] for every [illiberal] action". This is an example of the comprehensiveness, precision, and fecundity of the new paradigm.

> And his point on fraud no[t] being coercive is irrelevant because of the tie to property. One can not engage in fraud without engaging in misrepresentation of property ... whether that be money, one's person, or any object.

The *relevance* is that the *problem being discussed* was whether the absence of "coercion" is sufficient to characterise libertarianism. And in normal English such "misrepresentation" is neither an act of coercion (the use, or threat, of force to compel behaviour) nor aggression (the offensive use of force on a person).

Lester is then quoted (Lester 2014, chapter 10, p. 158-159):

> --- 'What about "aggression"? There seems to be no similar inherent problem with saying that libertarians are against aggression [...] The problem occurs when libertarians try to explain "aggression." For they then typically do so in terms of acts that flout legitimate property rights. There are really four mistakes in one here. First, as it stands, this view is compatible with every system of property: they are all perceived as "legitimate" from within themselves. Second, to some extent it appears to be circular: to simplify somewhat, aggression is flouting legitimate property and legitimate property is what is acquired without using aggression (and throwing self-ownership, "homesteading," and "labour-mingling" into the mix does not help). Third, there is a conflation of the factual and objective with the moral and legal: for it ought to be possible to say what libertarian liberty is—in theory and practice—without at the same time insisting that it is by its very nature "legitimate." Fourth, there is no independent theory of libertarian liberty from which it is possible to deduce what kinds of property are libertarian (whether or not they are "legitimate").' ---

The following response is made:

> I mean, really, is he joking? 'throwing self-ownership, "homesteading," and "labour-mingling" into the mix does not help'? Of course it does! These things are what allows for what property is!

This response does not relate to the *given discussion* of 'liberty' and 'aggression'. It is also false. 'Property', in the sense being discussed, is something to which someone has legal title. This does not entail how that title arose. And property is logically possible without assuming "self-ownership, "homesteading," and "labour-mingling".

> Admittedly they may or may not be the 'best possible' definition, but they are as logical and helpful as we have to this date.

They are not a "definition" of "property" at all. If applied, they give rise to a certain kind of property. How far that is libertarian is only possible to say with an independent theory of liberty. The way to refute a philosophical analysis is carefully to dissect it and show where the errors are. Instead, we are offered a reassertion of the very muddle that is being analysed.

> When he says
> --- 'The fundamental sense of "liberty" (or "freedom") that libertarianism implies is too abstract to be explained in terms of property—even self-ownership—first and foremost' ---
> this is precisely wrong! He is literally saying that liberty can not be explained. So how would [h]e explain this 'abstract' thing?

There is an explanation in the opening sections of chapter 10 of Lester 2014, which is just what is supposedly being criticised here. But it is often useful to try again. In any case, there is a difference between a Hobbesianesque approach and a Lockeanesque approach that also needs to be explained (this is not about what Hobbes and Locke actually wrote, but it resembles their contrasting fundamental approaches to liberty: each took one of the two main concepts of human liberty). In both cases here, this is considering what interpersonal liberty is in theory and what it entails in normal practice as matters of fact. The moral status of liberty is an entirely separate question that is not discussed: for it is an error to conflate the factual and the moral issues.

Arguments for Liberty

A pre-propertarian Hobbesianesque approach to interpersonal liberty

As we have seen, in terms of human actions a Hobbesianesque approach to interpersonal liberty is more or less zero-sum: if you have more interpersonal liberty, then someone else has less. A slave-owner qua slave-owner has more liberty where, and to the extent that, his slaves have less: whatever he can enforce that the slaves cannot prevent. Such zero-sum interpersonal liberty of action cannot be maximised or protected, it can only be competed over or redistributed for some non-libertarian reason (such as utility or equality). Therefore, it cannot be the liberty that most libertarians intend.

However, if the subjective intensities of interpersonal constraints are taken into account, then this does seem to allow for a libertarian interpretation (these aren't interpersonal intensities, beyond assuming that people are very broadly similar). For now interpersonal liberty can be interpreted as being free from all people-imposed constraints on our preference-satisfactions (that is, people don't stop us from getting what we want). If no one is constraining us in this way, then we have full interpersonal liberty. But people's preferences can clash. I might prefer to have you ultimately under my control; a 'slave', for short (although, strictly, slavery is a property concept). And you might prefer not to be my 'slave'. In the event of such clashes, the most 'libertarian' (i.e., liberty-observing) approach is to have whichever option is the lesser constraint. Almost universally, it is a greater constraint on one's preference-satisfactions to be someone's 'slave' than it is to be denied the possession of a 'slave'. If it were not, then people might take an evens gamble on being a 'slave' for the chance of having a 'slave'. But very few people would think that to be a prudent bet. People typically think that being made into a 'slave' would be a disaster. And not having a 'slave' is, at most, a relatively minor constraint (especially as trade is far more productive than having slavery). Therefore, such liberty is maximally observed if people have ultimate control of their own bodies (and their bodies are, more or less, what they are). This factual consequence is before the legal institution of property needs to be assumed. However, an efficient way to protect this ultimate control of one's body is then to assign property rights: to declare self-ownership.

A similar type of argument also applies to the control of all other resources. It is a greater constraint on our preference-satisfactions for other people to deny us ultimate control of resources we objectively possess (but do not yet own) by use or by voluntary transfer, than it is to be denied free access to all resources (especially as that would result in an immediate tragedy of the commons). Again, this factual consequence is before the legal institution of property needs to be assumed. But in order to better protect this control of such resources, it is efficient to have property rights.

In short, we can derive both self-ownership and private property (roughly, by initial use and thereafter voluntary transfer) because, contingently (for we can imagine worlds where this is not so), they maximally observe such interpersonal liberty. They are not what liberty is in theory, but what maximum liberty entails in practice. And once self-ownership and such property are thus derived from observing liberty, we can use those as rules as to what is 'libertarian' (that is, factually liberty-instantiating). It is only necessary to go back to the abstract theory of interpersonal liberty to answer philosophical questions or in occasional problem cases.

It is now possible to make an additional and separate ideological observation: as (almost) everyone's "rational" (that is, prudent) preferences lead in this direction, this then allows for a libertarian social contract on Hobbesianesque assumptions (and this is, more or less, Jan Narveson's approach).

A pre-propertarian Lockeanesque approach to interpersonal liberty

Here interpersonal liberty is interpreted as being free from peoples' *proactively*-imposed constraints on our preference-satisfactions (that is, people don't initiate interferences—whether intentionally or not—in our getting what we want). If no one is proactively constraining us in this way, then we have full interpersonal liberty. Now, if someone 'enslaves' me (i.e., proactively imposes ultimate control on me), then that is a proactive constraint on me, on what I am. He is not thereby exercising his interpersonal liberty, as here conceived, but exercising power or license over another person. And if I manage to prevent my 'enslavement', I am not proactively imposing on my would-be 'slave-owner', but merely reactively defending myself (the body that I, more or less, am) from him. Hence, ultimate control of oneself follows from observing such liberty. This factual and contingent consequence is before needing to assume the legal institution of property. But in order to better protect this ultimate control of oneself, we can institute self-ownership.

When it comes to external resources, matters are also slightly different. Once we have begun to use a resource for some purpose, then it typically proactively constrains us significantly if someone attempts to seize that resource from us. By controlling it, we might proactively constrain him too, but—more or less—only to the extent of the unmodified resource's value to him. For to be denied a benefit that someone else has somehow produced, is not to be proactively constrained (to simplify matters, this ignores discussion of costs relating to envy, lost status, frustrated desire, etc.). Therefore, it is typically a lesser proactive constraint on people's preference-satisfactions to allow ultimate control to the initial user (and thereafter control by voluntary transfer), than it is to have common access to all resources (and the consequent tragedy of the commons). This means that it maximally observes liberty to allow such personal ultimate control of external resources. This factual and contingent consequence is before needing to assume the legal institution of property. But in order to better protect liberty, it is efficient to have property rights in such resources.

In short, we can again derive both self-ownership and private property (roughly, by initial use and thereafter voluntary transfer) because, contingently (for we can imagine worlds where this is not so), they maximally observe such interpersonal liberty. They are not what liberty is in theory, but what maximum liberty entails in practice. And once self-ownership and such property are thus derived from observing liberty, we can use those as rules as to what is 'libertarian' (that is, factually liberty-instantiating). It is only necessary to go back to the abstract theory of interpersonal liberty to answer philosophical questions or in occasional problem cases.

Is one of these a better pre-propertarian approach to interpersonal liberty?

In light of these two explanations of interpersonal liberty, two questions immediately arise. Are these two approaches fully equivalent in terms of what they entail in practice? And is one to be preferred to the other for some reason?

Both conceptions of interpersonal liberty appear—at least initially—to have the same practical results. And, thus, one could explain interpersonal liberty using either. With the Hobbesianesque approach, we still have to say that a slave-owner is having his liberty lessened if his slaves are freed; just not as much liberty as his slaves gain by being freed. Similarly, a would-be person-killer has less liberty if his target-person escapes; just not as much as his target-person preserves his liberty by escaping that killing. This seems to be a logically coherent individualistic and egoistic approach (thereby, very roughly in accord with Hobbes's outlook). However, it is not how people mainly think about interpersonal liberty—either as self-described libertarians or otherwise. People tend to think about interpersonal liberty in the more social Lockeanesque way. They typically think that when someone escapes proactively-imposed control ('slavery'), he gains more liberty; but his previous controller ('master') has only lost his power or licence over him. And the would-be person-killer does not have his liberty lessened if his target-person escapes him; his target-person's liberty is simply preserved. Hence, it is closer to the main libertarian, and also more popular, approach to view liberty as the absence of people's proactively-imposed constraints on our preference-satisfactions (for short, no proactively-imposed costs). And where a complete absence is impossible (because there is a clash of proactive constraints: either you suffer the pollution of my fire, or I suffer having no warmth and no cooking) then liberty can only be maximised. It is very important not to misunderstand this final point. Dealing with clashes by *maximising* liberty might sound collectively consequentialist (at least, in some non-moral sense). However, that can't be right, for no one's liberty is curtailed in order to promote the maximum liberty of others in general. It's just that maximisation is all that is possible when specific liberties conflict.

All that said, we can now mention morals—but only to make a factual point. For the Lockeanesque conception of liberty seems significantly more morally attractive to people, as a matter of fact. And that fact probably means that it is more stable and less costly to preserve. Hence, more liberty will result. So that is one important practical difference, after all.

Nevertheless, there are—as mentioned—some Hobbesianesque libertarians (although they would probably not give the same precise account as here). Jan Narveson and Hillel Steiner are contemporary examples. And there are also anti-libertarians that take a Hobbesian approach to liberty. The late G. A. Cohen appears to be an example. So it is useful to be able to explain these two approaches. Doubtless, this important distinction could be further clarified and corrected, especially in response to criticisms. It is also possible that one of these approaches is in some way not logically coherent. In which case, it is good to have the other to fall back on. But if they are both logically incoherent, then that would mean starting again. For a tacit pre-propertarian conception of liberty seems necessary to distinguish forms of property that fit liberty from ones that don't. And so an explicit account should be possible.

Recapitulated criticisms

> I can not be more explicit than I have been […] so as a recap to reply to in bullet points -
> - one can not control what other people think and therefore by Lester's own words 'To own an "ideal object" (or abstraction, or meme) is to have control over its use' this actually CAN NOT BE SATISFIED BECAUSE ONE DOES NOT HAVE CONTROL OVER WHAT OTHER PEOPLE THINK. I thought scarcity was what you were not understanding but now think it must be this. If you can refute this bullet-point please do, but at least directly address it. Tell me how you can stop me thinking something.

Strictly, Lester should have written *"legal right of control over its use"*. And the flouting of a legal right does not mean that there is no legal right. Nevertheless, there are all sorts of practical limits on the protection of IP (as with physical property too: that cannot be perfectly protected either), but that does not undermine IP insofar as it is practical. Fortunately, it does not, in any case, appear to be a practical problem for IP that people merely think about someone's IP.

> - A theory of property can not be created without the use of some concept of liberty

Property is a legal right of use and control of something. Liberty doesn't need to be mentioned.

> and a theory of liberty can not be created without some use of the concept of property,

As we have seen at length, this is false.

> at the very least the property of one's own body (as Lester admits).

This was explicitly denied. That each person must have ultimate control of his body is first derived as a practical consequence of observing theoretical interpersonal liberty. Institutionalising this in law as self-ownership, for better protection, is a separate and further practical step.

> - The objective concept of property makes sense to apply in law because it is unequivocal in that it has physical boundaries.

Or intellectual boundaries, in the case of IP.

> There is no argument about whether I have infringed on your property if I move your physical property, or use it,

Or use IP without the owner's consent.

> - The subjective concept of 'proactive imposition' is impossible to determine since anyone can assert that any proactive action (any action at all) can impose on them under any circumstances.

For one thing, the concept of the reasonable person (as used in law) would need to be a practical limit on taking such assertions seriously. And so would the likely long-term consequences to liberty. However, the main answer is that—as has been explained—once certain types of property have been derived as practically instantiating theoretical liberty, then those types of property become libertarian rules. We would, at most, depart from them only if there were very strong evidence that liberty was not thereby being preserved. This can be understood as a sort of rule libertarianism as opposed to act libertarianism, but it is initially factual or positive (about what actually instantiates liberty) rather than moral or normative (an advocated principle). Apart from not being collectively consequentialist, it is analogous with the, well understood, distinction between rule utilitarianism and act utilitarianism.

Conclusion

As the above exchanges illustrate, the fundamental philosophy involved with mainstream libertarianism is a refuted and degenerating research programme. And the philosophy involved with the new paradigm is an unrefuted and highly fruitful one. The primary difference concerns fundamental philosophical distinctions. Where mainstream libertarianism has omissions, conflations, and circularities, the new paradigm explicitly distinguishes the following things: 1) abstract/theoretical interpersonal-liberty-in-itself: a) the non-normative and pre-propertarian absence of interpersonal proactive constraints on want-satisfaction, and b) that if clashes occur then such liberty can only be maximised, 2) practical/contingent derived applications of this: a) pre-propertertarian consequences, and only then (b) propertarian institutions, and 3) moral/rights issues. But a secondary significant difference is that mainstream libertarianism attempts various supporting justifications, while the new paradigm accepts that it is logically impossible to transcend a conjectural framework (for all observations, explanations, arguments, and even inferences, necessarily rest on assumptions) and so it uses the critical rationalist epistemology. However, despite these radical and important differences, new-paradigm libertarianism is not fundamentally ideologically at odds with libertarianism itself (although that is often the mainstream misperception). Consequently, the new paradigm could take the path of first being ignored, then ridiculed, then seriously criticised, and only finally accepted as significant theoretical progress within libertarianism. The final stage, at least, might require a new generation of libertarians.

Addendum: rebutting two further brief critical responses[3]

Responses to Sophie R's comments on the video-lecture:

Consider whilst watching if any of these questions were answered (which were Andy's key questions):

All of them were.

- A thought can not be practically scarce, or if so, how (other than it may only be thought of an amount of times equal to the number

> of people on the planet at any one given moment of time, which to me is hardly 'practically scarce')?

This isn't about thoughts; it's about abstractions. Each abstraction is one thing. Ownership of a particular abstraction is scarce, just as ownership of a particular piece of land is scarce.

> - Why should the right (in legal terms) of the thinker, who has willingly allowed his thought into the public ear, trump that of the practical man innovating this idea, with his own hands and property?

Property rights strongly tend to internalise externalities, especially if they are premised on doing just that. The owner tends to bear the costs and enjoy the benefits. This promotes economic efficiency: the optimal allocation of resources. It also promotes liberty: people not proactively constraining each other. This applies to intellectual property just as much as to physical property. It is arbitrary to presuppose that only physical property can be real property. To expect a "thinker" to keep his abstract products hidden or lose any property claim to them, is analogous with expecting a "practical man" to keep his physical products hidden or lose any property claim to them.

> - How can one define liberty

This isn't about a definition of the word 'liberty': how the word 'liberty' is used. It's about a theory of liberty: what interpersonal liberty is, both as an abstraction and what that abstraction entails when applied. Definitions are about the meanings of words; theories are about descriptions of the world. And the world includes the realm of all abstractions (which is also, incidentally, inhabited by all the entities of logic and mathematics). Philosophy cannot be done simply by looking in the dictionary, or providing a stipulative definition.

> without reference to property

Easily, apparently. There is no mention of property here, for instance: http://dictionary.reference.com/browse/liberty?s=t But the philosophical point is that it is coherent, and useful, to separate a theory of interpersonal liberty from any reference to property.

> without re-defining liberty as one could redefine any word? (Think Lenin and his 'first we confuse language' control technique.)

The irony here is that tendentious definitions are being used instead of answering philosophical arguments with philosophical arguments.

> - When in some arguments one decides that one owns oneself (as seems to be one of the foundational results within the definition of the age-old common conception of 'property' itself)

This seems to be asserting that the very "definition" (or is it a "conception"?) of "property" entails self-ownership. It would be interesting to see the argument. It seems to imply that slavery is either impossible or incoherent.

> and in other arguments define property and liberty in such a way as to reveal a deeming of self-ownership as making no sense,

Has anyone ever done that?

> how can this incongruity be reconciled?

Perhaps it can't. Is that a relevant problem?

> - Since 'ownership' of property - the thing that is protected by law - is that of having the ability to destroy that 'thing' (unless again we vastly redefine the English language),

Is there any dictionary that defines "'ownership' of property" to include "having the ability to destroy that 'thing'"? In any case, this would imply that no indestructible object could be owned.

> how can one destroy what Jan calls an 'ideal object'?

So that was another tendentious definition presented as being part of "the English language". Abstractions cannot be destroyed, of course.

> This also points to the term 'collective ownership' being an oxymoron to the point that one could own shares in something but no-one would have the right to destroy it.

It would depend on what any "collective ownership" contract said. Some destruction, under some circumstances, might even be obligatory.

> I have admitted that one could form a new level of 'property' that could be collectively shared, but this would not be ownership, the item would not be 'owned' by anyone at all.

Ownership exists to the extent that one has legal rights of use and control. Any number of people might share these with respect to any object, physical or abstract. What is forbidden, allowed, or compulsory as regards any destruction—or any other aspect—could be explicit in the relevant contract (but it might also be unclear and require arbitration to decide).

> - He keeps expressing how his thoughts are only theoretical and philosophical rather than practical and legal.

No. The theory of abstract interpersonal liberty is explicitly used to derive pre-propertarian practical implications and then propertarian legal ones. (A version of the text will appear in various places in due course.)

> This seems odd to me for two reasons, the first at base logical and the second a conjecture in passing: any correct and complete theory will 'work' in practice,

If a true theory has practical applications, then they must "'work' in practice".

> and is not the very use of both 'liberty' and 'property' in resultant concept deep-rootedly a practical matter?

Not all aspects of "'liberty' and 'property'" will involve a "practical matter". Not all philosophical aspects, for instance (such as thought experiments). But a large part of the purpose of moral, social, and political philosophy is to have practical implications.

> And if not, which from some angles may indeed be the case, is one not in the realm of 'personal ethics' shall we call it, rather than 'co-operative morals'?

There is no moral advocacy in the philosophical derivation of practical and propertarian conclusions from the abstract theory of liberty. By ironic contrast, the idiosyncratic and tendentious definitions (presented as being part of the "English language") are themselves "in the realm of 'personal ethics'"—with impractical consequences as regards intellectual property.

Responses to Andy Curzon's further comments:

> In response to this
> --- 'To expect a "thinker" to keep his abstract products hidden or lose any property claim to them, is analogous with expecting a "practical man" to keep his physical products hidden or lose any property claim to them.' ---
> it is not 'analogous' to any meaningful measure since abstractions are not practically scarce.

Each abstraction is only one abstract thing. The producer (discoverer/inventor/creator) of the abstraction can have one sole practical use for it (we may assume): to have a marketable property right in his product. That practical property-right use is scarce and rivalrous.

> If I can employ my scarce resources to build the result of your idea (an invention for example) then you do not lose the ability to use the idea, but if you use my pencil I lose the control of that pencil.

I "lose the ability to use the idea" as marketable property: the sole use (we may assume) for which I produced it.

> From my point of view an abstraction can not be controlled and as such may not be owned.

It is clearly possible to control the use of abstractions to a significant degree. That is what current IP law does now, albeit imperfectly with respect to a proper libertarian theory of liberty.

I think we shall have to agree to disagree on this one Jan! :)

"Thou know'st we work by wit and not by witchcraft,
And wit depends on dilatory time."
It also depends on seriously attempting to precisely fault any given arguments, rather than resorting to futile repetitions of the views that have been criticised. See what you think in a few years, Andy.

Notes

[1] Various private communications in recent years.
[2] See, e.g., Lester 2012, 95-105. Nozick suggests the same criterion with respect to patents, but based on an interpretation of the "Lockean proviso" (as he calls it) and "an adequate theory of justice" rather than an explicit theory of liberty (Nozick 1974, pp. 178-82).
[3] Both below the talk on youtube.com:
https://www.youtube.com/watch?v=75gZBwx_AYY

Bibliography

Lester, J. C. [2011] 2015. *Arguments for Liberty: a Libertarian Miscellany.* Buckingham: The University of Buckingham Press. Second, revised and expanded, edition.
——. [2000] 2012. *Escape from Leviathan: Libertarianism without Justificationism.* Buckingham: The University of Buckingham Press.
——. 2014. *Explaining Libertarianism: Some Philosophical Arguments.* Buckingham: The University of Buckingham Press.
Nozick, Robert. 1974. *Anarchy, State, and Utopia.* Oxford: Basil Blackwell.

33) Afterword and Further Reading

After many years of thinking, reading and writing about the nature and importance of interpersonal liberty, I find my theoretical understanding is significantly greater and my moral convictions are significantly stronger than when I started. And, on balance, the world itself has probably moved in a libertarian direction to a small but non-trivial degree. However, perhaps more important, there has been an efflorescence in the libertarian or classical liberal movement. Many more libertarian people, writings and activities are observable. And, consequently, even the authoritarians have been moving in a libertarian ideological direction to some degree. If I am right, then there is a critical ideological mass that we will approach, whereby libertarianism becomes the dominant ideology and this will lead to a relatively swift move to minimal states in some countries. With luck, that would be the beginning of the end for politics around the world. But all this will take time: at least many decades and possibly hundreds of years. It is important not to be impatient, for that might eventually lead to despair and a slowing of progress or possibly a reversal. Even merely to hold our current liberties is more than enough reason to continue with libertarianism's theoretical development, propaganda and other activities. But I do not doubt that we shall eventually see real progress as well. And that will be a better world for ourselves and our children.

There is almost no end of libertarian literature these days. The internet remains a burgeoning source, of course, and one that should be exploited. I mention below only a handful of possibilities that might be useful starting places for the journey.

Friedman, David D. [1973, 1989] 2015. *The Machinery of Freedom: Guide to a Radical Capitalism*. CreateSpace Independent Publishing Platform; 3rd edition.

Lester, J. C. [2000] 2012. *Escape from Leviathan: Libertarianism Without Justificationism*. Buckingham: The University of Buckingham Press.

———. 2014. *Explaining Libertarianism: Some Philosophical Arguments*. Buckingham: The University of Buckingham Press.

Narveson, Jan. 2008. *You and the State: A Fairly Brief Introduction to Political Philosophy*. Lanham, MD: Roman & Littlefield.

Rothbard, Murray N. [1973, 1978] 2006. *For a New Liberty: The Libertarian Manifesto*. Reissue of the revised edition. Auburn, AL: Ludwig von Mises Institute.